1

Mark Zupo

Achieve What You Can Believe, Believe What You Can Achieve!

Finding Success in self-empowerment

By

Mark Zupo

Zupo, Mark

Achieve What You Can Believe, Believe What You Can Achieve!

Finding Success in self-empowerment

ISBN-13:   978-0983994589 (Mark Zupo)

ISBN-10: 0983994587

Library of Congress catalog Card #

Also available in Audio, CD, & Kindle formats

To order, contact:

Mark Zupo

www.MarkZupo.com

SlipperyRock Press Publishing™

Acknowledgments

Most importantly, the first person to thank is my Mother. Expressing my gratitude to her would take this entire book and encompass every emotion known to man, so I will just offer the most sincere thanks a son can offer:

> *"All that I am and all that I hope to be,*
> *I owe to my mother."*
> **-Abraham Lincoln**

I would like to acknowledge all of the entrepreneurially- motivated people in the world, especially those who acted on their gut instincts, their visions of opportunity and their sense of independence. I would like to acknowledge anyone who ever had a brilliant idea or moment of inspiration when he thought could change the world. Those are the people who, because of their efforts to achieve more and succeed when the odds are against them, motivate me to success.

Mark Zupo

Introduction

There are two important differences between motivation and inspiration. It will become important to learn what they are and many more insightful reasons that will lead you to your success. I will teach you to understand why;

- You are the Master of Your Success
- You are the Master of Your Achievements
- You are the Master of Wealth, Freedom and Happiness

I believe that there are only three types of people:

1. The type of person that watches things happen
2. The type of person that makes things happen
3. and The type of person who asks, What happened?

<u>Which are you?</u>

I teach you how to dispel the myths of Failure, Lack of Control, and Negative Influences of Other People.

How to find your "Real Success System"

to empower you with the strength and desire to "Be All You Can Be" and "All You Want To Be!" If it's been done before, then You can do it too! Be The First To Imagine It, And then...Achieve What

You Can Believe!

Here, you will learn three simple goal setting methods that you can do before you are done brushing your teeth in the morning. How you can visualize your dreams and make them a reality. How you can do anything, be anything and achieve anything that anyone else can.

"Oh really" you say. Yes really! If it has been done before, someone just like you did it. So what makes you think that you can't do it? They had money, they had time, they had help, they had….who cares what they had! You have the same resources and that are within your reach and…all you have to do is ask for it.

When it comes to life and business, it is no coincidence that some people always seem to fail while others always seem to flourish. For sure, chance plays a role in everything. But as individuals, as business-owners, as thinkers, and as parents, we have a significant degree of control over our lives.

Now, we can use the control that we have to influence outcomes in bad ways. Or we can use it to influence outcomes in our favor; and in the favor of those we care about most.

When we use it poorly or when we don't use it at all, it should come as no surprise that our outcomes are bad. And when we use it thoughtfully and carefully, it should similarly be less surprising when we succeed.

Let me give you an example. At work, your employer considers you for a promotion; however, at the same time, she also considers several of your co-workers for a promotion, too. Now, as many do, you might immediately say —there's nothing I can do to influence my boss in my favor. Instead, this decision will be determined by things that are out of my control.ǁ And, of course, when the day comes, you will not get that promotion.

Instead, someone who pushed hard to demonstrate his worthiness for the position will get the job. And you will be left wondering why that person is always successful; and always gets promotions, raises, and the adoration of management.

You might even feel resentment towards that person, even though you consider him a friend. When it comes down to it, though, it wasn't your friend who caused you to miss the promotion (or at least not to give yourself the best shot at getting it). Rather, it was your own behavior that prevented your boss from seriously considering you as a candidate.

Fortunately for you, this book is all about situations just like the one we described above. It's about feeling powerless when you're not; experiencing bad outcomes when there's no reason to; and finally, it's about making sure this problem stops. Most importantly, this book is about success. It is about extracting the characteristics of others that make them successful at work, in parenthood, or in the workplace; and then adopting those characteristics for your own use.

So, without further ado, let's take the plunge. Today, you will stop telling yourself that you have no control over your life; and today, you will learn exactly what it means to take that control, grasp it firmly, and use it to achieve success in all areas of your life.

Set a goal, make a plan and DO IT!

I have always believed that you're destiny is determined when the decisions you make are put into action. I also believe that there is a greater power that guides your decisions. Ultimately, the path your life takes is directly proportional to the amount of education you have and the amount of labor you put into it. Some of the guidance you get is a direct link to your past experiences. Put your hand in the fire and you get burned. Chances are you will remember that lesson and not repeat the exercise and get burned twice just as in real life.

Most people have a set of rules they follow based on their experiences, education, wants, needs and desires. Those that choose to follow a path that they themselves question...usually leads to an end that was predictable and distasteful. With that in mind, you should follow the leadership of those who have succeeded before you by using their experiences, failures and successes as a guide to moving on your own ventures. As an example, watch someone else get burned and you will likely not repeat their actions in fear of the results you witnessed.

However, we strive to have what our neighbor has and sometimes more even if we really don't need it. We want to be like someone we respect and admire and are willing to change our life to accommodate that desire. That said, some questions come to mind;

√ **If there was one thing about your life that you could change...what would it be?**

This question comes with a bit of anticipation that when you adopt the change you will be better off than before. This answer is also laced with the indication that when the change is adopted it would lead to a better life, fame, fortune, notoriety, recognition, admiration or some other benefit that brings you to the forefront of other people's attention.

You should be warned though, this also come with risk, ambiguous results and undefined hazards. You will not be aware if the risk was worth the reward until after the change has been mad and then it may be too late to reverse. Kind of like going back in time to kill someone and accidently killing someone else in the process forever changing the history that was established before you left. This is very dangerous territory. To the point of that scenario, your motivation for success, freedom and wealth must be genuine and natural in order not to upset the balance of YOUR history.

The second question at hand is:

√ **When you found that one thing that you would change, what would stop you from doing it?**

Usually, we are held to our life history by the direction of our decisions and some opportunity.

Notice I didn't say luck. I believe that luck is the product of intuition, cognition, action and opportunity. I don't believe it is just happenstance. With that in mind, we have the ability to determine our course by some simple rules of intention. They are that we must:

- Achieve What You Believe Because You Believe you Can Achieve
- Know Thyself...and Thy Business Because You Are Your Business
- Build a Legacy Not a Reputation, one is Inheritable and the other is Despised
- Find The Message that Helps YOU Help Other People

The power of intention will be the driving force of your actions that determine your fate as a leader, an entrepreneur and a success in any endeavor in your life.

Part 1
Table of Contents

Achieve what you can believe

How to Keep Your Attitude in Check

Part 2
Table Of Contents

How to be genuinely happy

It's time to start a Healthy life

Make it happen be a leader

Meditation techniques

Motivation the heart of self improvement

Positive attitude can change the world around you

Self empowerment using people unlock your social potential

Self improvement and success

Start your own coaching

Take decision live your own life

The basics of goal settings

The power of relationships

Unleash your creative thinking

Unlock yourself improvement power

Time management and personal growth

What you should know on Leadership

Why is it important to improve yourself

Your 5 minute program to Stress management

Your 7 days program to Positive thinking

Mark Zupo

Your 7 days program to self improvement
Your 7 days program to Stress management

Part 1

Growth and Discovery

Know Thyself

We meet new people every day, for work or otherwise—whether we interact with them or not, you develops instinctive likes and dislikes towards people. This has lot to do with their personality.

To think that your personality is made up of only the way you look would be anomalous however. Your ideas, the way you think, your priorities in life, your emotions all comprise your personality. You need to understand and accept yourself the way you are if you want to be happy.

You can take a personality test to help you figure out what kind of personality you have. A substantial number of these are available online and in different books. Think about how much you know yourself. What are the things that are important for you? Put all societal and familial expectations aside for a minute and think about what you really want to do, what would make you happy? Knowing yourself well is important and will serve you well in various situations.

When you are looking for a job, for example, it would be ideal to not get stuck with something that you don't want to do. Knowing yourself would also help you accept other people as they are. It will help you develop an open mind.

One way or the other, the ultimate thing is to

do things that are important for you and that make you happy. If you are an introvert, you should regularly spend quality time by yourself. You can also keep your diary, if you are uncomfortable sharing your deeper thoughts with other people. Don't hesitate to stand by what you believe in.

This is important for you to be happy. It will be good for you to develop a constructive hobby. If you are introvert don't succumb to peer pressure and compulsively spend time with people. Learn how to say no. Draw lines around you and your space as and when you need to.

Extroverts on the other hand should get involved in group activities like theatre for example. Learn new things whenever possible. Don't hesitate to experiment. Stay in regular touch with your friends and family. If you have any introvert friends, learn to accept them as they are.

In your growing up years, a lot of things that are going on around you, go into shaping your personality. Some experts also believe that a lot of genetic factors go into making you who you are. But the important thing is to accept you the way you are.

If there are certain things about you that you don't like however, you can try to make minor alterations.

Discover Your Personality?

One of the most significant aspects of the modern world is the way you look and carry you. People are much inclined to appear like the movie stars or models of any fashionable person that they admire.

These famous personalities are considered to be paragons of fashion and beauty. But we always need to keep in mind that beauty is not just about wearing the right dress and looking hip. The most important factor that fashions beauty is your personality. We hardly look into this factor anymore. Once your personality is refined, you will have mastered eternal beauty.

Research reveals that men, often, prefer people who might not be very good looking but are sweet, interactive and trustworthy. Thus this shows that women who are not considered to be conventionally beautiful but have great personalities do attract a lot of attention. It is not a conflict between personality and good looks. Allow both these aspects in to mature simultaneously and you will notice that your personally will accentuate your good looks and vice versa.

Understand Yourself

The primary thing that you need to do is understand yourself. It is essential for you to comprehend your personality in order to refine it and thus improve your physical beauty. Let the process be slow and gradual.

You can also consult the various books and other content that is available – they will help you locate your character. Opt for the examinations as well as the help teams that are found on the test to know yourself better.

Each Person is Distinct and Special

One person can always consider another person's character and attitude in a negative light. Often people consider hyperactive or unusually quiet people to be crazy or odd. This notion is rather relative- each one appears little strange to another person. You can always utilize your attitude to improve yourself.

Supervising Your Virtues and Vices i.e. Your Features

Sort out your virtues and vices. Be a good person and get rid of all your negative points...

Focus on your virtues. If you wish to make your personality an instrument in order to be more appealing, then surely concentrate on your virtues and let your virtues be the attention centre. Each person is special and distinct in his or her own way. So let the good in you shine in front of others!

Personality is an essential component of the self of a person. By perfecting your personality you will be able to reveal the beauty that lies within you. Personality is not distinct from your external beauty. It is just an external manifestation of your internal splendor. It is important for you to let people understand that beauty is not just about good looks.

How Law of Attraction Helps in Personal Development

Laws of attraction can be very crucial when you are trying to understand your personality and its development. Failures and successes are a part of life and should be taken in the same spirit.

The ideal thing is to take all your failures as lessons for your life. Take these incidents to understand your limitations and things that you did wrong and try not to repeat them in the future. This is how you can pave the way for your success.

Deal with your failures as and when they occur. To keep them locked inside you and drag those along wherever you go will only complicate your present and future. What you think is what you are, is one of the most important laws of attraction. If you are always surrounded by negative, pessimistic thoughts it will hamper your growth and personality development.

Given below are some things you need to consider and sought out if you are working towards a positive personality:

Learn you accept yourself the way you are. You might have shortcomings and limitations but so does everybody else. If you can't love yourself, how will you love and accept other people. No matter how many things are going wrong around you, learn to take control. The moment start pitying yourself, you have lost half the battle already.

Even if you are surrounded by people who have a lot of negativity don't let it get to you. Try and make them see the brighter side of life if possible. But learn to step away as and when they start getting to you. No matter how messed up things are, tomorrow would be a new day and a new beginning. Stop mulling over your failures and try to fix things the best you can.

It's important to set goals for yourself. But make sure that the goals are realistic. Also reward yourself as and when you achieve desired results.

Learn to be confident about yourself. If you are sure about what you want go ahead and get it. Don't let anything put you down. Developing your personality means discovering your weaknesses and working on them. Learning from your failures and making sure that you don't commit the same mistakes again and again in crucial. Learn to be good to yourself and do things that make you happy. If you are good to people then you would *attract the same kind of behavior and people*. Learn to be positive and happy and everything will start to look up.

Do You Have A Positive Attitude?
Take the Quiz

This chapter presents the latest information on positive attitude. It is designed to either reconfirm your knowledge or enhance your knowledge on the subject by routing your thoughts on positive attitude through 5 questions.

1. Am I happy being where I am today?
This is a trick question without any standard answer, but knowing how to deal with it is crucial: for believing that you are happy can actually increase your happiness and contentment, and give you the confidence and positive attitude for anything that you wish to achieve. So do not simply wish to be happy but come out and believe that you really are: enjoy and be thankful for the little things in life and see what a difference it makes.

2. Am I appealing to the opposite sex?
Even if you do not have an answer to this, it shouldn't stop you from doing anything you wish. So be it shaping up, changing your dressing style or hairdo, your attitude towards people or life, do it as if you were appealing, and it shall conduce to your benefit. Remember that what matters the most is how well you can carry it off rather than exactly what you are trying to carry off.

3. How much could I have?

Operative here is not a standard that could define having too much or having too little, but rather how the question of how badly you really need or desire it. This boils down to asking yourself what, and how much, you are willing to work and sacrifice for something you think you want. If you really are willing to sweat for it, then no matter what, work on towards what you have set your heart on and the sky is the limit.

4. What motivates me?

Human desires are endless, and there are infinite variations to the things that make people happy. If you do not know what drives you or sets your pulse racing, approach life like a buffet service. Try everything piece by piece until you locate your favorite dish.

5. What Really Makes You Tick?

Understanding what really makes you tick is to not only be able to define your goal but also the path that you seek to chart towards that goal. So identify what you really want and what you are willing to do for it. It's all about knowing yourself; you own limits and doing your own cost benefit analysis, rather than any very profoundly philosophic quest.

Take Action!

The success (or failure) of your Internet Entrepreneurship really is up to you now. If you succeed, the credit will all belong to you and if you fail, you will own that as well. Your success or failure is in your own hands.

Success and failure are two sides of the same coin. The coin in question is your own Internet Entrepreneurship and you don't want to flip that coin into the air and leave it to chance as to whether it lands on success or failure. You want complete control over the fate of your Internet business and you do have that control.

Every decision will be yours to make. If you make wise choices then you will claim victory and success will be yours. If you make unwise choices then your internet business will crash and burn and your own hopes and dreams will go up in flames along with it.

Beating the Odds

You do realize, of course, that the odds for success are not in your favor. Every day thousands and thousands of internet business enterprises are launched. Of those internet businesses that will be launched today, 90% (ninety percent) will not be around in 120 days.

That is right! You have no better than a 10% chance of actually making a success out of your internet business unless you can change them those are not very good odds. If it were a horse race, winning would be considered a long shot.

That is the down side but anytime there is a down side there is always an upside. The upside in this case is that even though you have only a 10% chance at succeeding, you can greatly better your odds by simply following the guidelines that have already been offered. You can increase your odds from 10% to 90% by simply applying a few very simple principles to the problem. The reasons that so many new Internet entrepreneurs fail within the first 120 days can be narrowed down to four.

1. They do not have the right mindset.

2. They do not lay a solid foundation.

3. They do not have the key to unlock growth and expansion.

4. They do not plan for success

The Right Mindset for Success

Unfortunately, so many people think that they can quit their jobs, open an internet business and just relax and enjoy life. They expect instant success and instant wealth without having to invest anything (even time and effort) to affect that success.

They really believe that they can sleep until noon, work when and if they want to and just rack up sales and profit. This attitude probably accounts for at least half of all of the failures of new internet businesses. Making an internet business successful takes a lot of time and even more work. That old real world job demanded that you be on the job for probably 40 hours each week.

Your net internet business will need about twice that many hours each week if it is to become successful. Very, very, very few people are willing to invest that much time and effort thus the 90% failure rate. Of the few that are willing to put in enough time and effort most expect instant success.

They don't even consider the fact that they will need to continue to meet their own personal expenses for many months before they see the first penny of profit from a new internet business even though those facts are readily available. These are the ones who go out there looking for get-rich-quick schemes and end up becoming victims of internet scam artists.

The right mindset is this: You must expect to work hard. You must expect to work long and tedious hours. You will not be an over-night success. People are not going to line up to give you their money. You are going to have to earn it.

Your Business Success Depends on your Positive Attitude

Your business will prosper greatly if you build and consequently sustain a positive attitude. Even when things in your business are not going according to plan, you have to remember that you are not alone. All business ventures have their ups and downs.

Those impediments can be easily overcome and you can always get back on track if you keep a positive outlook to everything. You will also have increased confidence in yourself and your business capabilities. A positive attitude will make finding prospective customers simpler. Others will react well to your optimism. They will want to hire you and suggest you to others. This will also assist you in other departments of life. You will be in good health. Positive people have less fear of heart inflictions. Here are some useful tips for you to expand on your positive attitude.

- **Be Nice to Others:** Being polite and friendly with other individuals will make you feel nice about yourself. You will have a brilliant and happy day. However, you shouldn't be gullible and allow people to manipulate you because of your friendliness.

- **Mix with Other Positive People and Avoid Those who Have Negative Attitudes:** Attitudes rub on to others very quickly. If you spend more of your time with positive people you will automatically find yourself developing a more optimistic attitude.

However, negative attitudes can also be very infectious.

There is a popular saying which goes, "Misery loves company". When you are always in the company of people who perpetually complain, you will automatically find yourself beginning to do the same. Insignificant factors that would normally not bother you will suddenly seem to spoil your entire day. You will feel like you have lost all your energy. The moment you lose enthusiasm and incentive, it can prove very difficult to get back on track. These factors can take a negative toll on your business. You will not get anything constructive done this way.

- **Be Organized and Practice Time Management:** When you are systematic you will work faster and be able to complete more tasks. You will know exactly what you need to do achieve your target each day. You will do constructive work if you stay within a system instead wasting time searching for phone numbers or email addresses that you have misplaced.

- **Be Proactive:** The moment you are aware of an oncoming obstacle in your work, solve it instead of leaving it till the last instant. Be practical and have a solution ready before the problem can get out of hand. By being ahead of possible impediments, you will permanently be able to avoid setbacks.

- **Consider Hiring a Coach:** Many individuals hire tutors nowadays to attain success in business. These tutors of guides will assist you in deciding exactly what you require your business to yield. They will set attainable targets and will also demand justifications for actions.

Therefore, the right and positive attitude is the most important ingredient for a successful business. Practice it as well as follow it daily. You'll soon see you have become much more successful than you ever conceived of.

How You Can Master Success

The thing about starting a business...any business.....is that there is no guarantee of success under any circumstances.

Even big international businesses can fail at new business ventures. Failure is always an option but the possibility of success can be optimized.

You can optimize the possibility of success by:

1. **Having a good solid business plan in place BEFORE you launch your online business.** There is an old saying: "Those who fail to plan, plan to fail". A detailed set of plans for success needs to be made. You need to have the steps from getting from point A to point B listed in great detail that include realistic cost estimates for accomplishing each step.

2. **Expecting to work very hard to accomplish your goals.** You must never expect anything to be easy. You will be right

most of the time because things are rarely as easy as they look. Each step toward success requires work, time and patience. Sometimes things don't work out right on the first try. You have to be willing to try again and again until you do succeed.

3. **Not falling for 'get-rich-quick schemes.**
   The internet woods are full of those who prey upon those who are looking for quick and easy ways to become rich. Those ways do not exist. Get over thinking that there is an easy way. There is NOT.

Remember those statistics! Ninety percent of all new internet businesses fail in the first 120 days. You don't have to be part of that majority. You can become a part of that 10% minority of successful internet business enterprises.

Develop the Ideal Personality for Success in Business

A few days back when my associate informed me about this fresh advertising organization and also acquainted me with their webpage, I immediately looked into it. Well, it was absolutely detestable! It definitely had pretty pictures and a flashy look but the write up could hardly be read or understood. The webpage was designed craftily but was not a user friendly webpage.

The webpage was pathetic as it lacked a unique personality. It had no distinctive feature or that zing to hold my attention. The write up was quite uninteresting and so were the apparently lovely pictures. The write-up consisted of too many We's! The website lacked vitality and enthusiasm. It was a bit too perfect in its endeavor to impress all and thus could impress none!

People generally wish to conduct trade with people they have faith in and are fond of. You need to understand that people will be fond of you only

when your personality impresses them. There is no use at all concealing your true personality behind the veil of that silly, dull and dreary website! People will never get to be acquainted with you this way and they will also not wait for you for too long. According to Dan Kennedy, if you are dull and tedious in your advertising plans then it will lead you absolutely nowhere. No one will bother to pay you any attention if you are uninteresting. Most people will not even turn to look twice- there is so much more to do in life and so many other interesting things to look into!

Well these questions are now forming clouds in your mind: how will I work things out in case am not appreciated or in case I put off potential buyers? Well this might be the case with you and it probably should too. I shall explain why I incorporate the word "SHOULD".

The moment you are writing a note that is so sugar coated, you should immediately realize that it will be extremely dull and will attract none. In your endeavor to make it appealing, you will actually put off people. Your note will not incite any enthusiasm and hence you will not receive any clients. They would prefer someone who is adequately interesting.

Peter Montoya says that a nice label can excite people and also similarly fend them off. Hence if your organization is not resisting a certain crowd, then it is also not attracting your potential customers in a way it should.

Deter those people who would not be attracted to your personality or your commodities generally and yet wish to conduct business with you. Fend them off right from the start because they will never be fond of someone of your personality or be satisfied with your merchandise. It will never be a good deal!

Business is not just about formalities and official statements. This is the conventional view about business. You might be little apprehensive in the beginning but know that the more thrilling and stimulating your web content as well as write up is, the more popular will be the response to it. So you understand that your personality needs to blend in your label. Here you ask yourself "how do I go about this?" Well you will have to wait awhile- look into your inbox! I shall be giving you certain hints and suggestions in the upcoming copy.

Maintaining Positive Attitude

Successful people are identifiable by their masterful positive attitude, which makes it appear as if there's nothing that they couldn't achieve if they wanted and nothing they couldn't possess! It is a positive attitude which separates the successful from the losers: a self realized energy that propels towards success as opposed to a self defeating one that creates problems and provokes suffering in life.

Positive attitude is a state and condition of your mind that allows you to handle stress with optimism and patience, promoting hope and nullifying despair. This empowers you to be undeterred by problems, maintain your focus and continue to persevere without frustration, and thus eventually overcome all problems.

So if you have been a pessimist and have been filled with negative thoughts, here's how to get rid of your problem, embrace your cherished goals and develop a positive attitude.

1. **When you sense any signs of negativity or pessimism creeping into your mind, immediately check your thoughts and stop:** Instead try to imagine and visualize

your favorite memories, expectations or ideals.

2. **Experts recommend another way to banish negative thoughts from your mind, a mechanism which involves two basic stages:** The first which drives away negative thoughts and emotions, and the second which allows negativity to be infiltrated and overcome with positive thoughts and feelings.

3. **Talking to you and repeating positive affirmations are proven techniques to develop a positive mindset**. So devise your personal prep talk and motivation statement and make it a point to talk to yourself regularly.

4. **Another helpful way is to make posters or sticky notes carrying positive and affirmative statements such as: I can do it, Success is mine, My goal is within reach, etc, and to put them up around your home or workplace where you are apt see the message regularly, day and night.**

5. **Try to make the highly successful people be your friends and acquaintances, and**

try and spend time with them and know their approach. In the right company, it's easy for the secret to a positive attitude to rub off onto you.

6. **Begin to read positive self help books and magazine, or better still the biographies or autobiographies of your heroes.** You could also attend relevant seminars and workshops.

Remember that a positive attitude can only be cultivated and maintained by you; it is wholly internal to you which nobody can take away. It requires much time, effort and dedication, but is an invaluable asset.

Maintain a Positive Attitude During Hard Times

Often there are times when everything seems to go wrong despite one's hardest efforts. During these times, a positive attitude will assist a person to regain his stamina and come out of the rough patch easily.

You should never blame yourself for things that naturally seem to go wrong in life. These incidents cannot be avoided. You should always remember that tomorrow brings the hope of a new day.

Most days turn out to be positive for people, but there will always be occasional pitfalls when nothing seems to go right. Just take the failed day in your stride and move on ahead with the assurance that a better day will soon come.

Always let go of the distress of today and keep faith in the anticipation that tomorrow brings. Most of the days in an individual's life bring about positive results. If you can maintain a positive attitude regardless of what might happen, the bad days will be kept to a bare minimum.

Always remember that a positive attitude will help you recover quicker in times of distress. Some bad days will motivate you to have an even more positive attitude so that you can learn from the mistakes of today for a better tomorrow.

The situation may be extremely difficult. But a positive attitude will help you overcome irrespective of how bad the situation is and you will definitely regain your confidence and self respect.

Hard times will always appear in life. But they seem less hard when life is viewed optimistically. No matter how a hard life may seem at some stage, a positive attitude will help you keep your head clear and allow you to think steadily so that you can find the right solution.

Even at work, a positive attitude will help you

keep your calm and you will be able to do all the tasks that need to be done to improve the situation. You will be able to end your day on an optimistic note.

Even when you are sick or in despair, a positive attitude will help you recover quicker. The illness or the disappointment will pass sooner. You should not break down simply because you don't feel fit and fine. Real strength and stamina come from learning to be optimistic and believing that time will soon change for the better. No one is flawless. Making mistakes is a natural part of life. You have to learn from your wrongdoings and be prepared for the future. You should not always blame yourself and lose your composure when something goes wrong. Make this a positive learning opportunity for the future. It is easy to maintain a positive attitude during smooth times. It is only when you can do

the same during rougher times that you can achieve happiness and success much faster.

Using Your Attitude As Your Ally

It may seem easy to just make your attitude your ally. You probably will not need a lot of convincing to at least give it a try. What do you have to lose? If you are used to letting your attitude lead you, then it is something you are already familiar with.

People make their attitude their ally all the time. Most of the time they do it without even realizing it. Unfortunately, most of the time the attitude is a negative one. It is often easier to see how a negative attitude acts as an ally than how a positive attitude acts as an ally. This is just human nature to see negative over positive. We are more often drawn to drawing out the negative over the positive. Pessimistic attitudes seem to flood the world, while optimism is slowly drowning.

You can probably come up with many examples of how negative thinking or a negative attitude has turned into a negative situation. You can probably point out negative people and give plenty of examples how that negative attitude is influencing their life.

You may even be able to look at your own life and see how negativity has affected you. It's likely you have let a negative attitude direct you in at least one situation in your life.

Can you remember a time when your negative attitude caused problems in a situation? You can probably look at it now and see just how the negative attitude worked against you. Even if the situation was not a positive one to begin with, your negative attitude likely comes into play.

While this can teach you about how your attitude can become your ally, it also teaches you that you want to do everything possible to make sure your attitude is positive. If you really want to make your attitude your ally and you want that ally to be positive, then you need to start looking at the positive. You have to train your mind to find the positive in everything. You have to ignore the negative. Take the negative you cannot ignore and turn it into a positive. Your ally does not need to be crowded with negativity.

Imagine your ally. An ally filled with negativity is crowded. There are road blocks and other things that get in your way or cause you to not be able to walk the path you choose. You may even have to work to get around these negative things.

If your ally is positive, then it is filled with positive things. There are no roadblocks that you cannot handle. Anything that falls in your way is easy to get past. With an ally filled with positive things you will find that it is easy to travel and that you can get past anything that may come into your path.

You can clearly see that a positive attitude is much better than a negative attitude. You would, obviously, rather have an ally that is easy to get down, than one filled with things that get in your way and slow you down. Using your attitude as your ally involves many levels of changing your life. You will have to change things you daily, through your interactions with other people, your thoughts and your goals.

As mentioned, the way you shape your thoughts and goals will go a long way towards helping you shape your attitude and making your attitude your ally. Make sure you make a conscious effort to keep these things positive.

When you interact with other people you are basically broadcasting your attitude. You want this to always be positive. People will react to you in a positive manner if you approach them in a positive manner. Your interaction with others is very important in your life. You want those interactions to be positive. This will allow you to bring positive things into your life. A good example is during a job interview. If you approach the interview with a negative attitude then you likely will not get the job.

Go to the same interview with a positive attitude and you have a better chance of getting that job. The way you approach others can have a huge impact on your life, so make sure you are using your attitude as your ally when interacting with others. Your attitude should be your ally every day. It will take some time to make it routine. In the beginning, you will likely have to work hard to make sure you are being positive in every aspect of your life. You will have to make an effort to stay positive and to think positive. It can be difficult, especially if you often give in to negative thoughts and actions.

It is also common when you approach a situation in a positive manner that you end up having a positive experience. People are more likely to help you and to go out of their way to make sure you get what you need when you approach things in a positive manner. So with your attitude as your ally, you are opening yourself up to a lot of positive experiences.

Using your attitude as your ally is about making everything in your life positive. That means associating with positive people, keeping yourself in positive situations and surrounding yourself with positive things.

You have to get rid of negativity. You have to start being positive about everything. By doing this, you are creating your ally. You are paving your road with the positive and this will lead you to positive results.

What You Need to Be on the Top

Have you noticed a certain kind of radiance and aura surrounding people who are successful and doing well in their lives?

Some people have one particular skill that they tap on for their success while some people have a whole range of plus points that work in their favor in their professional life and otherwise. It's important to identify things that you are good at and concentrate on them and to know how to work them in your favor.

Especially with regards to your professional life, it's important that you should be doing something that you truly love. If you are not sure about what it is that you really want don't be afraid to experiment. Look around. Spend time doing things that you haven't done before. This will also enable you to discover your strengths, weaknesses and interests. Before everything else, you need to identify what success means to you.

Largely speaking there are two spheres in which people seek to be successful—personal (relating to friends and family) and professional (relating to your field of work). Some skills are however useful for both these spheres.

It's important how you react to and act upon emotions. It's important to maintain your cool in all kinds of stress-ridden situations. People who maintain their calm are most likely to make logical decisions be in control.

Failures are a part of life. Learn to take them in your stride. It is ideal to learn from your mistakes. The key to success is that you should stop being afraid of failures. If you have a goal in your mind you have to persistent. Don't give up. You have to be innovative and think out of the box. When faced with a problem retain your cool and think of all possible ways to tackle it. Don't be afraid of fear. You might be afraid of doing new things and taking new challenges or of pushing yourself to new limits. This would also limit your success. Use your fear constructively. The curiosity might have killed the cat but it is good for you.

Ask questions, when you are not sure about what is happening. It's important for you to get a clear picture of the happenings before you can even identify the problem and then eventually tackle it.

If you want to be successful, you need to inculcate level headedness patience. You need to be willing to learn from people around you and keep an open mind. Don't be afraid to do new things and think beyond conventional framework.

Traits of a Dynamic Personality

The right attitude not only defines who you are but also your stance and success in life. That is why all top of the line business owners are those who have in their lives been not just about physical, mental and social prowess, but about the right attitude, with regards to the nature of success and achievement and the need to achieve something in life. Some of the primary qualities of a successful man are listed below for your perusal.

1. **Powerful need to achieve** — This quality is not the entrepreneur's quantitative success score card about how much has been done. Neither is this just about gaining popularity through success. It is the basic need to do something in life to make it worthwhile to oneself and gain self respect in the eyes of others.

2. **Perseverance** — Getting an inspiration, no matter how vague, and standing by it to see the resultant end through, is a primary characteristic of a success story. This never-admit-defeat and always-be-determined aspect is the most defined stamp of a dynamic personality.

3. **Positive mental attitude** —There is nothing that speaks of success in a person more than his optimistic mindset. Every successful person

4. has to endure hard times and challenges and this is the time when his optimism carries him forth.

5. **Objectivity** — Knowing one's self, knowing ones shortcomings and carrying on accordingly, without getting emotionally affected is also a must have quality in a successful person. This will not only enable him to assess the pros and cons of a certain move matter of fact, but will also enable him to, without personal involvement, stand by or discard a project according to its qualities.

6. **Foresight** — Any successful person must have a gift of vision. This vision is not the divine or spiritual vision but the gift of anticipation and foresight. This quality if possessed allows a person to always b on guard and aware of all possible occurrences where business is concerned.

7. **Well-developed personal relations skills** — You are nothing without your clients and

partners in any business venture. That is why being a people person, without overt involvement, is absolutely crucial for any successful business man.

8. **Strong communication skills** — You have ideas and you need to convey it to others to make it a reality. But conveying does not mean that it will be accepted, so convincing has to be added to it. This is Why the ability to communicate confidently, both on pen and paper and by word of mouth, is extremely important.

9. **Resourcefulness** — Instinctive ability to foresee problems and solve them, even though it is a never-heard-of-before-kind, is also a quality of the successful man. It hints at the ability of being aware and draw inspiration from immediate surroundings to deal with the matter at hand.

10. **Technical knowledge** — The know-how of your field, be it the technical aspect or the economic is extremely important for a businessman, this will enable him to be ahead of all situations and deal with possible problems in a well rounded manner.

11. **A respectful attitude towards money —**
The ability to not equate money with success
but with the means to do something
worthwhile is very important. This ensures
that the successful man remains more than a
mercenary at the end of the day and still
appreciates the value of hard work and
diligence.

So here in a nutshell are the qualities that make a
man a living success story...do you have it in you to
be one?

Innovative Thinking and Passion

One thing that has not been mentioned yet is
about the role passion plays in innovative thinking.
It is true thought. You have to have passion about
your innovative ideas or you will never get
anywhere with them. You have to feel strongly that
your ideas are worthy. You have to believe in
yourself and know that your ideas are good. IF you
do not stand behind your ideas, then it will be quite
hard to get others on board with them. Being
passionate about innovative ideas is not something
that you can learn. It is something that comes from
the heart. It is something that is uncontrollable.

You have to be able to tell others about your
innovative idea and get them excited. It is
impossible to do that if you do not have any

passion about your product.

It is hard to develop passion.

However, if you immediately feel very strongly about an idea you come up with, then chances are it is something worth going with. When you have that immediate passion about something then it is natural and it really is something you believe in.

It is your job to make sure people know about your passion for your idea. It is hard to argue with someone or put down their idea if they seem so passionate about it. Let people know that you really do care about your idea and that you will not be quick to let them push it aside. Persistence and passion go together when it comes to inventions and ideas. People are quick to ignore or put off things that are new. People will likely not be nearly as interested in your idea as you are, so you have to be ready for that.

You have to keep pushing your idea in front of people. It is the passion that will drive you to do this. So never let go of the passion. Never allow yourself to lose your fight and drive. Always stand behind your idea. Always know what to say – be prepared. When people come at you with negative remarks or even questions, then you have to be available to answer back. You need to know the ins and outs of your idea and you have to be able to explain every detail so you can talk to others about it.

Do not forget about passion when it comes to innovative thinking. If you forget the passion then you will likely end up never getting your idea recognized for the brilliance they are.

Learn to Face Criticisms

Everyone has faced some kind of criticism at some point in their lives for sure. No one in their sane head would call criticisms as fun. Rather they can turn out to be quite discouraging. You must keep a very positive attitude when it comes to criticisms. For doing this you must be aware of the two vital areas from where every form of criticism usually generates.

Those Who Truly Believes in You and Want to Help You Out

This is the type of criticism that usually hurts the most. Nobody likes the fact that you are being criticized by the people whom you love and respect the most. However one must keep their intentions in mind. If someone is really close to you and want the best to happen to you, they would not sweet talk you for your mistakes.

When your closest ones criticize it is usually a constructive criticism and you must pay heed to that and if you feel that it is for your best interest then follow their suggestions and imply the adjustments they might offer.

Those Who Do Not Have Your Best Interest at Heart

This form of criticism can come as a surprise or might blindside you. This type of criticisms usually comes from people whom you never thought important or never knew that they were keeping a tab on your life.

Though some of the times these criticisms do pay off but most of the times it is best not to pay any kind of attention on what they have to say. Even if you are right and doing something positive and great there will be people who will come and criticize your work.

In both the above mentioned examples keep in mind that your attitude should not under any circumstances be affected by the criticisms. Maintaining a constant positive attitude is a lot like when it rains outside. Just because it is raining outside does not necessarily imply that you would have to sit inside the room. Rather you put on a raincoat or take an umbrella and go outside in spite of the rain. Similarly if criticisms starts showering upon you do not let that stop you from achieving any goal that you have set for yourself in your life. You must keep a positive outlook. Maintaining this positive attitude would help you in keeping the criticisms out of your life.

Personality Style Differences Between Managers and Leaders

Managers and leader serve two distinct and separate functions within any organization. It is therefore important to keep in mind the required difference in the personality styles of these two roles. The chief purpose of a manager is to ensure the proper operation of administrative processes in an organization and to thereby maximize its productive output.

A manager is required to maintain stability, discipline and control in the organization, and to solve problems with a view to the given operational structure, resources, goals and employee benefit. They are required to manage the problems that need to be resolved and optimize performance given the organizational restraints and to devise the best ways to do so.

Managers therefore tend to base their decisions more on the pressing and immediate needs of the day rather than long term goals and objectives. Since they must necessarily focus on the current states of activities their decisions may often appear narrow; but it is also possible for them to look upon their work as an enabling process rather than one meant only for damage control. So, on their part, managers are good at working out short term strategies, negotiating compromises and mediating conflicts.

They can make valuable decisions by maneuvering people and ideas and by organizing and balancing contrary people and points of view. Leaders, on the other hand, are generally conceived of as successful but lonely individuals. They have attained mastery over themselves and therefore can better control others while also creating for them a vision which infuses their work with value and direction.

Leaders are accordingly held to be imaginative, fervent and prone to taking risks; they are perceived to be proactive for promoting their ideas instead of simply reacting to the present situation.

They shed new light on long-standing problems and are engaged in developing their ideas and solutions. Similarly, leaders are seen as possessing the ability to relate to people in intuitive and empathetic ways, and to fill them with enthusiasm for their ideas. Thus, a leader tends to be a new arrival to an organization, someone who has been imported for their vision, daring and innovation, but who may not necessarily have the experience or worldly prudence to implement the motion of change.

So whereas a leader is one who can instinctively command a following amongst employees and unite them for a common goal, a manager has to steadily work up the ladder and seek authority on the basis of their rooted and proven position in the company. A manager has to gain his standing through long and dependable service and effective organizational skills based on a clear understanding of how each level of the organization works.

Thus, managers and leaders adopt different approaches towards their goals. While the leader uses passion to generate emotion, the manager utilizes a more formal, rational method. But irrespective of these differences, successful managers and leaders both must seek to motivate and involve their employees.

If they can make the employee believe that he is appreciated and respected, and is a significant part of the organization, it is that much easier to inspire him and tap his potential.

Therefore it is vital for managers and leaders to involve employees in the process of making decisions and to inform them of any changes relevant to their position. Additionally, it is important for managers and leaders to remain approachable and available to employees and to show genuine interest in their needs. All this generates a sense of security and belongingness in employees, making them wants to work harder and contribute to the overall success of the organization.

Do You Have The Personality To Innovate?

The difference between an idea generator and a successful innovator lies in the latter's ability to undertake what is called "kaleidoscopic thinking". The first step towards creating a culture within the organization which is conducive to the fomenting of innovation is to identify employees who have

the gift of kaleidoscopic thinking. We present nine traits which could help you identify the innovator amongst your people:

- **Curiosity is the basic component in innovation,** which makes the person question the status quo, seek new approaches and explanations and devise new solutions and pursue new possibilities. Not limiting themselves to the superficial aspect of things, they probe delve, imagining novel alternatives and paradigms.

- **Risk-taking and critical thinking**. But simply a curious and imaginative mentality does not an innovator make. It is necessary to be able to embrace risk and to be able to recognize the real possibilities of failure. Our experience with a number of our clients who are evaluating their leadership succession strength has revealed that many experienced managers, who have had to work their way up the ladder, become averse to risk with increasing stakes.

- **Resilience and Self-Control.** It is necessary that an innovation driven culture clearly acknowledge and build its function around the fact that many attempted innovations shall meet with failure. Many managers simply can't digest that, trying to negate any attendant risk and seeking a 95% guarantee that the proposed idea is actually going to hit off. this kills off rather than promotes innovation.
- **Interpersonal Skills**. Great innovative projects often frizzle out due to the failure to coordinate and communicate around the idea. This happens when the organizational charge is in the hands of the best techies rather than the best leaders. These technically oriented managers suppose that the innovative idea will automatically generate interest and motivation, and when they do try and communicate they do not try to attune their language to the sensibilities of their audiences, leaving them mystified.

- **Collaboration.** Innovate requires collaboration and teamwork. This is not a project specific endeavor but a spontaneous and continuous aspect of the work ethic. Best innovation proceeds from collective brain storming and a coordinated approach.
- **Dealing with Problems and Evolving Continually.** A final key element is the ability to handle complexity and adapt accordingly without wasting undue time. It is imperative to be able to meet up to the constant shifts and dynamism of the markets and the challenge of competition. Innovation is incomplete if it doesn't match up to and outpace the competition, and if contingencies throw projects off track.

Assessing the actual preparedness for change and the conduciveness to innovation in your organization are necessary before declaring your company to be innovation driven. For if you do not have the proper people and the right environment to implement your business plan, your innovative vision will remain a dream.

The Key to Continuous Growth and Expansion

Grow or die! This is one of the laws of nature that applies to all living things. All business lives by this law as well. A business cannot begin, grow to a certain point and then simply remain at that point and continue to thrive.

Growth and expansion are necessary for the business to survive and if that growth and expansion do not happen then the business will fade and die or crash and burn. Growth and expansion of business must be controlled by the business owners or managers. If growth is too slow, the business lags behind the competition. If growth is too fast, the business can easily become over extended. A steady controlled growth is the ideal. Of course, the ideal and the reality are sometimes two very different things.

Sometimes the terms 'growth and expansion' are a bit misunderstood. The most obvious meaning of both terms is to get bigger and broader but those meanings are not the only ones that apply.

Growth, for example, can mean gaining knowledge and becoming wiser and expansion can mean broadening the knowledge base from which a company operates.

A small internet based company does not have to grow and expand until it becomes a giant multi-national company in order to survive but the owners and managers of these internet businesses do have to grow by getting smarter and expand by welcoming change with open arms.

Nothing ever just stays the same. Change is

the only certainty in the world. What was hot or what worked yesterday is old news today and it will be ancient history tomorrow.

Companies and company owners and managers must grow with and adapt to changes as they happen and on the internet changes happen a lot faster than they do out in the brick and mortar world.

We all agree that growing, adapting and expanding is vital to the survival of any business and maybe especially to Internet business. So the question is: What is the key to growth and expansion of internet based businesses?

When brick and mortar businesses grow and expand, they build bigger buildings and hire more employees but that isn't exactly an option for an internet based business.

The key to growth and expansion of an internet based business is for the business owner or manager to always and continuously invest in them.

They must be willing to stay on the cutting edge of technology and they must be willing to accept and adapt to changes as they occur. Internet businesses are not buildings. Internet businesses are people. An internet business cannot grow by investing in a larger building. It only grows when the person who is driving that business invests in his or her own knowledge and ability. An internet business cannot expand by investing in hiring more people. An internet business expands when the person who is driving it invests in himself or herself.

The bottom line is this: The key to continuous growth and expansion of an internet based business is continuous investments being made in the owner or manager of the business. The short answer:

Invest in Yourself

You have no doubt heard this refrain many times. But what does 'invest in yourself mean'? Does it mean you should go out and invest in a haircut that costs two hundred bucks? Does it mean that you should go by yourself a designer suit? What does it mean to invest in yourself?

Well, if you can afford it, go get that haircut and buy that designer suit but that is not the kind of investment that we are talking about here. Your internet business is just you, your computer and your internet connection and you could actually operate your internet business from any commuter on the planet that had an internet connection.

So basically, your business is really only you. Your business is based only upon your own knowledge and your own ability. Those are the 'company' assets and those are the ones that need to grow and expand constantly so that your internet business thrives. Here is a rule that you might want to live by to insure that your internet business is a success and continues to be a success: Invest 5% of your time and income into improving yourself.

Expansion and growth are imperative to survival and expansion and growth of an internet business means expanding and growing the knowledge of the person running the company...that would be YOU. A tiny investment of only 5% of your time and your income per year in yourself can mean that you will continue to see positive monetary returns for many, many years to come. You might be sitting there shaking your head and still wondering what is meant by a 5% time and income investment per year in yourself. What is meant is that you must expand your knowledge.

You must stay on top of new technological advancements and you must expand your knowledge base about your own area of expertise. Things change fast. New information becomes available on almost everything under the sun every day of the week.

It is very, very easy to fall behind very, very quickly. And unless you consciously put forth the effort to stay on top of things you will most certainly fall behind. Keeping up is easier than catching up and if you keep up, you can usually find a way to forge ahead.

Yes, you are so busy right now that you could

use 48 hour days but taking just about one hour per day out of the 24 that you are allotted and only $5 out of every hundred dollars that you earn and investing that time and money in yourself can increase your future earnings a hundred fold.

There are newsletters, webinars, Tele-seminars and real brick and mortar seminars that can provide information and cause your knowledge to grow and expand so that your business can also grow and expand but you must be willing to invest in yourself so that you can take advantage of this information...learn it...and apply it to your own internet business.

Live An Action Driven Life

Did you know that people who live an action oriented life do things in a different manner? Unlike 'normal' people, they are truly passionate about what they are doing and they will do whatever it takes because they want it bad. They want it so bad that they can't sleep at night until they achieve it.

Imagine that you are a teenage boy or a girl. You have met your first love and you want him or her so bad. If your mom or dad told you that you cannot leave the house, what would you do if you really want to see him or her? Would you sneak out at night? Would you climb out the window and slip away? You would do whatever it takes, right?

That's exactly the way action driven people do things!

Whether you identify with this or not, it remains a known fact that if you want to accomplish your goals real bad, you have to live the following characteristics:

- **You have to believe in what you are doing.**

No one would believe in you if you do not believe in yourself! If you don't have a firm belief in your mission, then who the heck is going to carry it out for you? They don't even know what your mission is! Like a rebellious teenager, you can't change them unless they truly want to change themselves!

- **You also have to develop a compelling desire to get things done.**

Like the example above, having a compelling desire is very important because if you don't have a compelling desire, most of the time, you will go halfway and later on, 'no way' because you will lose your drive.

You must have a plan.

- **If you do not have an effective plan, you will fail after awhile.**

Even with a strong belief and a compelling desire, you will still fall flat on your face and you will be confused because you want it so bad yet you can't get the results. A man without a plan is simply in dreamland.

- You must do whatever it takes all the way...
- You must have an iron will that is even stronger than Ironman's armor!

What will you do when you feel down? Are you going to live in defeat? With these 4 traits, you will have the strength to live an action driven life!

Keep a Check on Your Attitude

It is quite a decent idea to keep a check on your attitude regularly. Certain attitudes must be checked; noticed and rectified otherwise they become our philosophy, which is dangerous.

Let's check some common attitude problems.

Anger

Anger is an inflated view of one's self and attitude. Arrogance makes one deaf about other people's feelings, ideas or feedbacks. Arrogance is really a showcase of what we lack- genuine confidence. Genuine confidence gets you closer to other people arrogance takes you away.

Solution: God has given you three wonderful gifts- appreciation, confidence and humility. Practice them and you will go a long way.

EOE – Instant Expert On Everything

This is a person who has the answers to

everything and is ready to speak about it at length (or a know-it-all). IEOEs can be difficult to train or teach. Any relationship with this person, whether a friend, co worker or spouse is quite difficult. Ignorance is what you get if you are such a person.

Solution: Try developing a sense of curiosity for the world and its operations. Learn to say "I don't know" and then find answers.

Refusal of Taking Responsibility for Your Own Actions

If you do not take responsibility of your actions then it is a moral or emotional problem. If we do not take responsibility the power of changing things is also lost. Blaming others give them the power to change things and eradicate your problem-solving abilities.

Solution: when you are in trouble ask these three questions- What can I do? What can I read or know about? Whom shall I consult for expertise?

AAMS- the All about Me Syndrome

This is simply selfishness personified. There's a big difference between self care which is caring about one's self and being selfish which is me first and to heck with the rest. Usually children have this behavior because it is natural during development. Growing up, means realizing that we are not the center of the universe.

Solution: Maintain a balance between taking care

of you and noticing other people's lives and emotions.

Minimizing the Seriousness of Your Effect on Others

It is very easy to not notice what influence we are drawing up on others. If you are in any form of relationship what you do directly affects the other people around you. Not only your work but also your belief affects them.

Solution: Go back and see how others decisions have affected you. Then reflect on your actions and how they would have affected others.

Skill and Development

Table Of Contents

How natural medicine can help you

How to be genuinely happy

It's time to start a Healthy life

Make it happen be a leader

Meditation techniques

Motivation the heart of self improvement

Positive attitude can change the world around you

Self empowerment using people unlock your social potential

Self improvement and success

Start your own coaching

Take decision live your own life

The basics of goal settings

The power of relationships

Unleash your creative thinking

Unlock yourself improvement power

Time management and personal growth

What you should know on Leadership

Why is it important to improve yourself

Your 5 minute daily program to Stress management

Your 7 days program to Positive thinking

Your 7 days program to self improvement

Your 7 days program to Stress management

Your secret to success

10 Questions you should ask yourself

"What Really Makes You Tick?" 10 questions you should ask to yourself: a preparation to self-improvement

Be all you can be, but it's not always in the Army. I often see myself as somewhat contented with my life the way things are, but of course it's hard to think of anything else when where are real issues to be discussed. Still I aspire for something deeper and more meaningful.

So we're all pelted with problems. Honestly it shouldn't even bother or even hinder us to becoming all we ought to be. Aspirations as kids should continue to live within us, even though it would be short-lived or as long as we could hold on to the dream. They say you can't teach an old dog new tricks... or can they?

1. What do I really want?
The question of the ages. So many things you want to do with your life and so little time to even go about during the day.

Find something that you are good at can help

realize that small step towards improvement. Diligence is the key to know that it is worth it.

2. Should I really change?

Today's generation has taken another level of redefining 'self', or at least that's what the kids are saying. Having an army of teenage nieces and nephews has taught me that there are far worse things that they could have had than acne or maybe even promiscuity. So how does that fit into your lifestyle?

If history has taught us one thing, it's the life that we have gone through. Try to see if partying Seventies style wouldn't appeal to the younger generation, but dancing is part of partying. Watch them applaud after showing them how to really dance than break their bones in break-dancing.

3. What's the bright side in all of this?

With so much is happening around us there seem to be no room for even considering that light at the end of the tunnel. We can still see it as something positive without undergoing so much scrutiny. And if it's a train at the end of the tunnel, take it for a ride and see what makes the world go round!

4. Am I comfortable with what I'm doing?

There's always the easy way and the right way when it comes to deciding what goes with which shoes, or purse, shirt and whatnot. It doesn't take a genius to see yourself as someone unique, or else we'll all be equally the same in everything we do. Variety brings in very interesting and exciting questions to be experimented.

5. Have I done enough for myself?

Have you, or is there something more you want to do? Discontentment in every aspect can be dangerous in large doses, but in small amounts you'll be able to see and do stuff you could never imagine doing.

6. Am I happy at where I am today?

It's an unfair question so let it be an answer! You love being a good and loving mom or dad to your kids, then take it up a notch! Your kids will love you forever. The same goes with everyday life!

7. Am I appealing to the opposite sex?

So maybe I don't have an answer to that, but that doesn't mean I can't try it, though. Whether you shape-up, change the way you wear your clothes or hair, or even your attitude towards people, you should always remember it will always be for your own benefit.

8. How much could I have?

I suppose in this case there is no such things on

having things too much or too little, but it's more on how badly you really need it. I'd like to have lots of money, no denying that, but the question is that how much are you willing to work for it?

9. What motivates me?

What motivates you? It's an answer you have to find out for yourself. There are so many things that can make everyone happy, but to choose one of the may be the hardest part. It's not like you can't have one serving of your favorite food in a buffet and that's it. Just try it piece by piece.

10. What Really Makes You Tick?

So? What really makes you tick? You can be just about anything you always wanted to be, but to realize that attaining something that may seem very difficult is already giving up before you even start that journey. Always remember, that self-improvement is not just about the physical or philosophical change you have to undergo, but it's something that you really want.

10 Ways to empower your communication

"A Piece of Blarney Stone" 10 ways to empower your communication

The Blarney Stone is a historical stone, or actually part of the Blarney Castle in Ireland where it was believed that kissing the stone can grant you the gift of gab. Yeah, it seems strange in this day and age, but who are we to question tradition? It's not like I'm saying that Santa Claus doesn't exist (OOPS!).

There is so much to know about conversation that anyone, even I, could ever realize. You can go though watching talk shows; radio programs; clubs dedicated to public speaking; ordinary conversations; certain rules still apply when it comes to interaction through words. It may sound tedious, I know, but even though it's your mouth that's doing the work, your brain works twice as hard to churn out a lot of things you know. So what better way to start learning to be an effective communication is to know the very person closest to you: yourself.

1. What you know.
Education is all about learning the basics, but to

be an effective speaker is to practice what you've learned. My stint as guest at every Toastmasters' meeting I go to taught me that we all have our limitations, but that doesn't mean we can't learn to keep up and share what we know.

2. Listening.

It's just as important as asking questions. Sometimes listening to the sound of our own voice can teach us to be a little bit confident with ourselves and to say the things we believe in with conviction.

3. Humility

We all make mistakes, and sometimes we tend to slur our words, stutter, and probably mispronounce certain words even though we know what it means, but rarely use it only to impress listeners. So in a group, don't be afraid to ask if you're saying the right word properly and if they're unsure about it then make a joke out of it. I promise you it'll make everyone laugh and you can get away with it as well.

4. Eye Contact

There's a lot to say when it comes to directing your attention to your audience with an eye-catching gaze. It's important that you keep your focus when talking to a large group in a meeting or a gathering, even though he or she may be gorgeous.

5. Kidding around

A little bit of humor can do wonders to lift the tension, or worse boredom when making your speech. That way, you'll get the attention of the majority of the crowd and they'll feel that you're just as approachable, and as human to those who listen.

6. Be like the rest of them

Interaction is all about mingling with other people. You'll get a lot of ideas, as well as knowing what people make them as they are.

7. Me, Myself, and I

Admit it, there are times you sing to yourself in the shower. I know I do! Listening to the sound of your own voice while you practice your speech in front of a mirror can help correct the stress areas of your pitch. And while you're at it you can spruce up as well.

8. With a smile

A smile says it all much like eye contact. There's no point on grimacing or frowning in a meeting or a gathering, unless it's a wake. You can better express what you're saying when you smile.

9. A Role Model

There must be at least one or two people in

your life you have listened to when they're at a public gathering or maybe at church. Sure they read their lines, but taking a mental note of how they emphasize what they say can help you once you take center stage.

10. Preparation

Make the best out of preparation rather than just scribbling notes and often in a hurried panic. Some people like to write things down on index cards, while other resort to being a little more silly as they look at their notes written on the palm of their hand (not for clammy hands, please). Just be comfortable with what you know since you enjoy your work.

And that about wraps it up. These suggestions are rather amateurish in edgewise, but I've learned to empower myself when it comes to public or private speaking and it never hurts to be with people to listen how they make conversations and meetings far more enjoyable as well as educational.

10 Ways to start taking control

"Who's the Boss?" 10 ways to start taking control (time management, goal setting, record tracking)

At first glance, it would seem that positive thinking and Attention Deficit Disorder (ADD) have nothing to do with one another. But many of us with ADD develop negative thinking patterns because we become frustrated by our challenges and frequent feelings of being overwhelmed. This negative outlook then makes it even harder for us to manage those challenges and move forward.

Practicing positive thinking allows people with ADD to focus on our strengths and accomplishments, which increases happiness and motivation. This, in turn, allows us to spend more time making progress, and less time feeling down and stuck. The following tips provide practical suggestions that you can use to help you shift into more positive thinking patterns:

1. Take Good Care of Yourself
It's much easier to be positive when you are eating well, exercising, and getting enough rest.

2. Remind Yourself of the Things You Are

Grateful For

Stresses and challenges don't seem quite as bad when you are constantly reminding yourself of the things that are right in life. Taking just 60 seconds a day to stop and appreciate the good things will make a huge difference.

3. Look for the Proof Instead of Making Assumptions

A fear of not being liked or accepted sometimes leads us to assume that we know what others are thinking, but our fears are usually not reality. If you have a fear that a friend or family member's bad mood is due to something you did, or that your co-workers are secretly gossiping about you when you turn your back, speak up and ask them. Don't waste time worrying that you did something wrong unless you have proof that there is something to worry about.

4. Refrain from Using Absolutes

Have you ever told a partner "You're ALWAYS late!" or complained to a friend "You NEVER call me!"? Thinking and speaking in absolutes like 'always' and 'never' makes the situation seem worse than it is, and programs your brain into believing that certain people are incapable of delivering.

5. Detach From Negative Thoughts

Your thoughts can't hold any power over you if you

don't judge them. If you notice yourself having a negative thought, detach from it, witness it, and don't follow it.

6. Squash the "ANTs"

In his book "Change Your Brain, Change Your Life," Dr. Daniel Amen talks about "ANTs" - Automatic Negative Thoughts. These are the bad thoughts that are usually reactionary, like "Those people are laughing, they must be talking about me," or "The boss wants to see me? It must be bad!" When you notice these thoughts, realize that they are nothing more than ANTs and squash them!

7. Practice Lovin', Touchin' & Squeezin' (Your Friends and Family)

You don't have to be an expert to know the benefits of a good hug. Positive physical contact with friends, loved ones, and even pets, is an instant pick-me-up. One research study on this subject had a waitress touch some of her customers on the arm as she handed them their checks. She received higher tips from these customers than from the ones she didn't touch!

8. Increase Your Social Activity

By increasing social activity, you decrease loneliness. Surround yourself with healthy, happy people, and their positive energy will affect you in a positive way!

9. Volunteer for an Organization, or Help another Person

Everyone feels good after helping. You can volunteer your time, your money, or your resources. The more positive energy you put out into the world, the more you will receive in return.

10. Use Pattern Interrupts to Combat Rumination

If you find yourself ruminating, a great way to stop it is to interrupt the pattern and force yourself to do something completely different. Rumination is like hyper-focus on something negative. It's never productive, because it's not rational or solution-oriented, it's just excessive worry. Try changing your physical environment - go for a walk or sit outside. You could also call a friend, pick up a book, or turn on some music.

When it comes to the corporate world, protocol is pretty much the religion. To know the things needed to do are the basics of productivity, but interaction and having a steady mind makes up the entire thing to true productivity. There are those who seem to work well even under pressure, but they're uncommon ones and we are human and imperfect. To get these little things like stress under our skins won't solve our problems. Sometimes it takes a bit of courage to admit that

we're turning to be workaholics than tell ourselves
that we're not doing our best.

Be as happy as You Want to Be

Almost everyone have heard the hit single 'Don't Worry, Be Happy' by Bobby McFerrin. The song has a very catchy way of conveying its message of being happy to everyone. Bobby McFerrin's simple message surely made a lot of people by telling them not to worry.

Living a happy, resilient and optimistic life is wonderful, and is also good for your health. Being happy actually protects you from the stresses of life. Stress is linked to top causes of death such as heart disease, cancer and stroke.

One of the better things ever said is - 'The only thing in life that will always remain the same is change', and in our life we have the power to make the necessary changes if we want to. Even if we find ourselves in an unbearable situation we can always find solace in the knowledge that it too would change.

Social networks or relationships are essential to happiness. People are different, accept people for who or what they are, avoid clashes, constant arguments, and let go of all kinds of resentments. If arguments seem unavoidable still try and make an effort to understand the situation and you might just get along with well with Happiness is actually found in everyone, increasing it is a way to make a life more wonderful and also more healthy.

To be happy is relatively easy, just decide to be a happy person. Abraham Lincoln observed that most people for most of the time can choose how happy or stressed, how relaxed or troubled, how bright or dull their outlook to be. The choice is simple really, choose to be happy.

There are several ways by which you can do this. Being grateful is a great attitude. We have so much to be thankful for. Thank the taxi driver for bringing you home safely, thank the cook for a wonderful dinner and thank the guy who cleans your windows. Also thank the mailman for bringing you your mails, thank the policeman for making your place safe and thank God for being alive.

News is stressful. Get less of it. Some people just can't start their day without their daily dose of news. Try and think about it, 99% of the news we hear or read is bad news. Starting the day with bad news does not seem to be a sensible thing to do.

A religious connection is also recommended. Being part of a religious group with its singing, sacraments, chanting, prayers and meditations foster inner peace. Manage your time. Time is invaluable and too important to waste. Time management can be viewed as a list of rules that involves scheduling, setting goals, planning, creating lists of things to do and prioritizing. These are the core basics of time management that should be understood to develop an efficient personal time management skill. These basic skills can be fine tuned further to include the finer points of each skill that can give you that extra reserve to make the results you desire.

Laugh and laugh heartily every day. Heard a good joke? Tell your friends or family about it. As they also say -'Laughter is the best medicine'. Express your feelings, affections, friendship and passion to people around you. They will most likely reciprocate your actions. Try not to keep pent up anger of frustrations, this is bad for your health. Instead find ways of expressing them in a way that will not cause more injury or hurt to anyone.

Working hard brings tremendous personal satisfaction. It gives a feeling of being competent in finishing our tasks. Accomplishments are necessary for all of us, they give us a sense of value. Work on things that you feel worthy of your time.

Learning is a joyful exercise. Try and learn something new every day. Learning also makes us expand and broaden our horizons. And could also give us more opportunities in the future. Run, jog, walk and do other things that your body was made for. Feel alive. Avoid exposure to negative elements like loud noises, toxins and hazardous places.

And always remember the quote from Abraham Lincoln, he says that, "Most people are about as happy as they make up their minds to be."

Bring innovation into your life

What Innovation Can Do to Your Life

It's a talent that everyone has, yet they think they don't. The power of innovation. If you've ever marveled at somebody's creative prowess, guess what, you can create and innovate too. It just takes time. Everyone is born creative. The box of crayons in kindergarten were not limited to those who possessed potential; because the truth is, everybody has potential.

You know how long it took to learn to ride a bike or drive or to never commit the same mistake again? It's the same with innovation. It takes a bit of practice and a lot of time before this mind function comes easily when called. This article will teach you a few tips on how to bring innovation into your life.

Don't listen to what other people say. Follow the beat of your own drum. Allowing for the input of other people will only bring cacophony to the music you are trying to make. If you have an original idea, don't waste your time and effort trying to make people understand. They won't. And the help you will probably get comes in the form of negative feedback. If all those geniuses listened to their peers, we would probably still be living in the middle ages.

Spend time on it.

I cannot stress that enough, although, please do not mistake this tip to tell you to quit your day job entirely. Do not. This involves some tricky time management but with a little discipline you'll be able to squeeze both in.

Exercise. Take a walk.

Run a mile or two. Send all those endorphins coursing through your veins. Exercising certainly clears and relaxes your mind and allows for anything to pop up.

Record your dreams.

Aren't some of them just the craziest things that your conscious mind would never have thought of? If you've had these dreams before, and I'm sure have, this only shows you the untapped innovative power you have lying within. So jot down those notes. Those dreams may just create an innovative spark in you.

Find your own style.

You can always tell a Van Gogh from a Matisse. You'll know Hemingway wrote something by the choice of words on the paper. So it is the same with you. People will appreciate your innovation more because it is uniquely yours and that no one else would have thought of what you were thinking.

That will let people see how valuable an asset you are.

Don't hide behind nifty gadgets or tools.

You don't need the most expensive set of paints to produce a masterpiece. The same way with writing. You don't need some expensive fountain pen and really smooth paper for a bestseller. In fact, J.K. Rowling wrote the first book of the Harry Potter Series on bits of tissue. So what if you've got an expensive SLR camera if you're a crappy photographer? Who cares if you've got a blinging laptop if you can't write at all? The artist actually reduces the number of tools he has as he gets better at his craft: he knows what works and what doesn't.

Nothing will work without passion.

What wakes you up in the mornings? What keeps the flame burning? What is the one thing that you'll die if you don't do? Sometimes people with talent are overtaken by the people who want it more. Think the hare and the tortoise. Ellen DeGeneres once said that if you're not doing something that you want to do, then you don't really want to do it. And that's true. Sometimes you just want something so bad you become a virtual unstoppable. And that is passion. Passion will keep you going.

Don't worry about inspiration.

You can't force it; inspiration hits when you least expect it to, for those unpredictable yet inevitable moments you should prepare. An idea could strike you on the subway, yet alas, you poor unfortunate soul; you have no sheet of paper to scribble down a thought that could change the world. Avoid these disasters. Have a pen and paper within your arm's reach at all times.

Build your self esteem a starter guide to self improvement

BUILD YOUR SELF ESTEEM, A STARTER GUIDE TO SELF IMPROVEMENT

So how do you stay calm, composed and maintain self esteem in a tough environment? Here are some tips you may to consider as a starter guide to self improvement.

Imagine yourself as a Dart Board. Everything and everyone else around you may become Dart Pins, at one point or another. These dart pins will destroy your self esteem and pull you down in ways you won't even remember. Don't let them destroy you, or get the best of you. So which dart pins should you avoid?

Dart Pin #1 : Negative Work Environment

Beware of "dog eat dog" theory where everyone else is fighting just to get ahead. This is where non-appreciative people usually thrive. No one will appreciate your contributions even if you miss lunch and dinner, and stay up late. Most of the time you get to work too much without getting help from people concerned. Stay out of this, it will ruin your self esteem. Competition is at stake anywhere. Be healthy enough to compete, but in a healthy competition that is.

Dart Pin #2: Other People's Behavior

Bulldozers, brown noses, gossipmongers, whiners, backstabbers, snipers, people walking wounded, controllers, naggers, complainers, exploders, patronizes, sluffers... all these kinds of people will pose bad vibes for your self esteem, as well as to yourself improvement scheme.

Dart Pin #3: Changing Environment

You can't be a green bug on a brown field. Changes challenge our paradigms. It tests our flexibility, adaptability and alters the way we think. Changes will make life difficult for awhile, it may cause stress but it will help us find ways to improve our selves. Change will be there forever, we must be susceptible to it.

Dart Pin #4: Past Experience

It's okay to cry and say "ouch!" when we experience pain. But don't let pain transform itself into fear. It might grab you by the tail and swing you around. Treat each failure and mistake as a lesson.

Dart Pin #5: Negative World View

Look at what you're looking at. Don't wrap yourself up with all the negativities of the world. In building self esteem, we must learn how to make the best out of worst situations.

Dart Pin #6: Determination Theory

The way you are and your behavioral traits is said to be a mixed end product of your inherited traits (genetics), your upbringing (psychic), and your environmental surroundings such as your spouse, the company, the economy or your circle of friends. You have your own identity. If your father is a failure, it doesn't mean you have to be a failure too. Learn from other people's experience, so you'll never have to encounter the same mistakes.

Sometimes, you may want to wonder if some people are born leaders or positive thinkers. NO. Being positive, and staying positive is a choice. Building self esteem and drawing lines for self improvement is a choice, not a rule or a talent. God wouldn't come down from heaven and tell you – "George, you may now have the permission to build self esteem and improve yourself."

In life, it's hard to stay tough specially when things and people around you keep pulling you down. When we get to the battle field, we should choose the right luggage to bring and armors to use, and pick those that are bullet proof. Life's options give us arrays of more options. Along the battle, we will get hit and bruised. And wearing a bullet proof armor ideally means 'self change'. The kind of change which comes from within. Voluntarily. Armor or Self Change changes 3 things: our attitude, our behavior and our way of thinking.

Building self esteem will eventually lead to self improvement if we start to become responsible for who we are, what we have and what we do. It's like a flame that should gradually spread like a brush fire from inside and out. When we develop self esteem, we take control of our mission, values and discipline. Self esteem brings about self improvement, true assessment, and determination. So how do you start putting up the building blocks of self esteem? Be positive. Be contented and happy. Be appreciative. Never miss an opportunity to compliment. A positive way of living will help you build self esteem, your starter guide to self improvement.

Coaching: an easy way to make things happen

Why Coaching is the Way to Go in Team Management

When you hear the word "coach", what comes first into your mind? Do you picture a basketball team with a man/woman shouting out directions? Or perhaps a football team with a man/woman pacing to and fro and calling out the names of the players?

Coaching is no longer reserved to sports teams; it is now one of the key concepts in leadership and management. Why is coaching popular?

Coaching levels the playing field.

Coaching is one of the six emotional leadership styles proposed by Daniel Goleman. Moreover, it is a behavior or role that leaders enforce in the context of situational leadership. As a leadership style, coaching is used when the members of a group or team are competent and motivated, but do not have an idea of the long-term goals of an organization. This involves two levels of coaching: team and individual. Team coaching makes members work together. In a group of individuals, not everyone may have nor share the same level of competence and commitment to a goal. A group may be a mix of highly competent and moderately competent members with varying levels of commitment. These differences can cause friction among the members. The coaching leader helps the members level their expectations. Also, the coaching leader manages differing perspectives so that the common goal succeeds over personal goals and interests. In a big organization, leaders need to align the staffs' personal values and goals with that of the organization so that long-term directions can be pursued.

Coaching builds up confidence and competence.

Individual coaching is an example of situational leadership at work. It aims to mentor one-on-one building up the confidence of members by affirming good performance during regular feedbacks; and increase competence by helping the member assess his/her strengths and weaknesses towards career planning and professional development. Depending on the individual's level of competence and commitment, a leader may exercise more coaching behavior for the less-experienced members. Usually, this happens in the case of new staffs. The direct supervisor gives more defined tasks and holds regular feedbacks for the new staff, and gradually lessens the amount of coaching, directing, and supporting roles to favor delegating as competence and confidence increase.

Coaching promotes individual and team excellence.

Excellence is a product of habitual good practice. The regularity of meetings and constructive feedback is important in establishing habits. Members catch the habit of constantly assessing themselves for their strengths and areas for improvement that they themselves perceive what knowledge, skills, and attitudes they need to acquire to attain team goals. In the process, they attain individually excellence as well. An example is in the case of a musical orchestra: each member plays a different instrument. In order to achieve harmony of music from the different instrument, members will polish their part in the piece, aside from practicing as an ensemble. Consequently, they improve individually as an instrument player.

Coaching develops high commitment to common goals.

A coaching leader balances the attainment of immediate targets with long-term goals towards the vision of an organization. As mentioned earlier, with the alignment of personal goals with organizational or team goals, personal interests are kept in check.

By constantly communicating the vision through formal and informal conversations, the members are inspired and motivated. Setting short-term team goals aligned with organizational goals; and making an action plan to attain these goals can help sustain the increased motivation and commitment to common goals of the members.

Coaching produces valuable leaders.

Leadership by example is important in coaching. A coaching leader loses credibility when he/she cannot practice what he/she preaches. This means that a coaching leader should be well organized, highly competent is his/her field, communicates openly and encourages feedback, and has a clear idea of the organization's vision-mission-goals. By vicarious and purposive learning, members catch the same good practices and attitudes from the coaching leader, turning them into coaching leaders themselves. If a member experiences good coaching, he/she is most likely to do the same things when entrusted with formal leadership roles.

Some words of caution though: coaching is just one of the styles of leadership. It can be done in combination with the other five emotional leadership styles depending on the profile of the emerging team. Moreover, coaching as a leadership style requires that you are physically, emotionally, and mentally fit most of the time since it involves two levels of coaching: individual and team. Your members expect you to be the last one to give up or bail out in any situation especially during times of crises. A coaching leader must be conscious that coaching entails investing time on each individual, and on the whole team. Moreover, that the responsibilities are greater since while you are coaching members, you are also developing future coaches as well.

Develop your intuition

The Road to Intuition

Have you had that experience when all of a sudden you just had this huge hunch that something is about to happen, and to your surprise, that intuition was eventually translated to reality?

When you feel strongly about something without logical basis to it, that's called intuition. It comes in three impressions: clairvoyance or "the third eye", sensing clearly and feeling through listening.

Clairvoyance is when your eye goes beyond what it can see. This is when you know what is happening somewhere.

Sensing clearly is basically what we refer to as "hunch" or "gut feel." This is the time when you are overwhelmed with a feeling and you can't explain it and all you can say is "I just know."

On the other hand, feeling through listening or clairaudience is being able to "listen" between the lines. Intuition also happens at times when a certain sound, whatever it is - be it a car's honk or a bird's twitting - ushers in an intense feeling.

They say only a number of people are gifted with intuition. Astrologers even insist that people born under the Scorpio or Pisces signs are naturally intuitive it almost borders on E.S.P. But studies have been sprouting left and right that proclaim that anyone can develop intuition.

Why the need to develop intuition, you ask? Why not let your emotional and psychological state as it is? First and foremost, intuition promotes good communication. It makes you more sensitive to the people around you; it often keeps you from hurting those you love because you are intuitive enough to understand them. Intuition also makes you far more creative than ever. Intuition means releasing more creative juices for any means of expression. Lastly, intuition has a healing power. This healing power is not in the physical sense, but in delving deep into your soul to eradicate some negative energy buried in it.

With that being said, are you ready to develop your intuition? Here are some ways to unlock this gift:

1. Hypnosis

Oh yes, get yourself hypnotized. Hypnosis is not limited to watching a pendulum move back and forth. Perform self-hypnosis or you can avail of hypnotic programs that can strengthen your intuition.

2. Meditation

Meditating means finding peace in yourself. If your mind and heart are cluttered with too many baggage and hurt, you wouldn't be able to quiet down that part of you that could eventually initiate intuition. There are so many ways to meditate: take a yoga class, or just simply practice some breathing that could bring you straight to Zen.

3. Think positive!

A worry-free, fear-free state could do so much to improve your intuitive ability. By staying positive, you attract good energy that would be able to easily recognize imminent feelings and events.

4. Just let go.

What does this mean? If you are on the brink of making a huge decision, let go of all the inhibitions and head to a quiet place where you could find out where the letting go has brought you. Sometimes you just have to listen to the voice within you, and that voice wouldn't come out unless you let go.

5. Never expect.

After letting go of the inhibitions and all those things that stop you from thinking and feeling clearly, never expect for an answer right away. Never expect that the "hunch" would fall on your lap immediately. Give it a little time then you'd just get surprised that -- wham! -- now you have your answer.

6. Believe in your first impressions.

When you see someone for the first time and think that he is a bit too arrogant for your taste, chances are that impression actually holds true. Most of the time, first impressions are brought by intuition.

7. Stay happy!

See? All you need to be intuitive is to stay happy! Happiness attracts immense power and such power includes intuition. In tapping your intuition, your motivation must be happiness and contentment. Given that premise, intuition will fall to you easily.

Intuition is helpful, because sometimes it leads you to something that cannot be achieved otherwise. A lot of lives have been saved by intuition alone. Decisions are easier done if armed by this gift. Develop intuition now and reap benefits you have never imagined.

Dream your life

Impossible is Just a Word

Everyone, at some point of his or her life, has dreamed of being somebody special, somebody big. Who hasn't fantasized about being the one who hits the game-winning homer? Who hasn't dreamed of being the homecoming queen? And how many times have we dreamed of being rich, or successful, or happy with our relationships?

Often, we dream big dreams and have great aspirations. Unfortunately, our dreams remain just that – dreams. And our aspirations easily collect dust in our attic.

This is a sad turn of events in our life. Instead of experiencing exciting adventures in self actualization, we get caught up in the humdrum of living from day-to-day just barely existing.

But you know what? Life could be so much better, if only we learned to aim higher.

The most common problem to setting goals is the word impossible. Most people get hung up thinking I can't do this. It's too hard. It's too impossible. No one can do this.

However, if everyone thought that, there would

be no inventions, no innovations, and no breakthroughs in human accomplishment.

Remember that scientists were baffled when they took a look at the humble bumblebee. Theoretically, they said, it was impossible for the bumblebee to fly. Unfortunately for the bumble, bee no one has told it so. So fly it does.

On the other hand, some people suffer from dreaming totally outrageous dreams and not acting on them. The result? Broken dreams, and tattered aspirations.

If you limit yourself with self-doubt, and self-limiting assumptions, you will never be able to break past what you deem impossible. If you reach too far out into the sky without working towards your goal, you will find yourself clinging on to the impossible dream.

Try this exercise. Take a piece of paper and write down some goals in your life. Under one header, list down things 'you know you can do'. Under another header, write the things 'you might be able to do.' And under one more, list the things that that are 'impossible for you to do.'

Now look at all the headers strive every day to accomplish the goals that are under things 'you know you can do'. Check them when you are able to accomplish them. As you slowly are able to check all of your goals under that heading, try accomplishing the goals under the other header-the one that reads 'you might be able to do.'

As of the items you wrote under things I could do are accomplished, you can move the goals that are under things that are 'impossible for you to do' to the list of things 'you might be able to do.'

As you iterate through this process, you will find out that the goals you thought were impossible become easier to accomplish. And the impossible begin to seem possible after all.

You see, the technique here is not to limit your imagination. It is to aim high, and start working towards that goal little by little. However, it also is unwise to set a goal that is truly unrealistic.

Those who just dream towards a goal without working hard end up disappointed and disillusioned.

On the other hand, if you told someone a hundred years ago that it was possible for man to be on the moon, they would laugh at you. If you had told them that you could send mail from here to the other side of the world in a few seconds, they would say you were out of your mind. But, through sheer desire and perseverance, these impossible dreams are now realities.

Thomas Edison once said that genius is 1% inspiration and 99% perspiration. Nothing could be truer. For one to accomplish his or her dreams, there has to be had work and discipline. But take note that that 1% has to be a think-big dream, and not some easily accomplished one.

Ask any gym rat and he or she will tell you that there can be no gains unless you are put out of your comfort zone. Remember the saying, "No pain, no gain"? That is as true as it can be.

So dream on, friend! Don't get caught up with your perceived limitations. Think big and work hard to attain those dreams. As you step up the ladder of progress, you will just about find out that the impossible has just become a little bit more possible.

Enjoy your life change your point of view

Enjoy Your Life: Change Your Point of View

"Two men look out through the same bars: One sees the mud, and one sees the stars."- Frederick Langbridge, A Cluster of Quiet Thoughts

If you've placed second in a writing contest, will you jump for joy and push for better results the next time or will you be discouraged and find an excuse not to join again?

In life, you are always filled with choices. You may opt to have a pessimist's view and live a self-defeated life or you may decide to take the optimist's route and take a challenging and fulfilling life.

So why nurture an optimist's point of view? And why now?

Well, optimism has been linked to positive mood and good morale; to academic, athletic, military, occupational and political success; to popularity; to good health and even to long life and freedom from trauma.

On the other hand, the rates of depression and pessimism have never been higher. It affects middle-aged adults the same way it hits younger people. The mean age of onset has gone from 30 to 15. It is no longer a middle-aged housewife's disorder but also a teen-ager's disorder' as well.

Here's how optimists are in action and researches that back up why it really pays to be an optimist:

Optimists expect the best

The defining characteristic of pessimists is that they tend to believe bad events, which will last a long time and undermine everything they do, are their own fault.

The truth is optimists are confronted with the same hard knocks of this world. What differs is the way they explain their misfortune---it's the opposite way. They tend to believe defeat is just a temporary setback, that its causes are confined to this one case.

Optimists tend to focus on and plan for the 'problem' at hand. They use 'positive reinterpretation.' In other words, they most likely reinterpret a negative experience in a way that helps them learn and grow. Such people are unfazed by bad situation, they perceive it is a challenge and try harder.

They won't say "things will never get better," "If I failed once, it will happen again" and "If I experience misfortune in one part of my life, then it will happen in my whole life."

Positive expectancies of optimists also predict better reactions during transitions to new environments, sudden tragedies and unlikely turn of events. If they fall, they will stand up. They see opportunities instead of obstacles.

People respond positively to optimists

Optimists are proactive and less dependent on others for their happiness. They find no need to control or manipulate people. They usually draw people towards them. Their optimistic view of the world can be contagious and influence those they are with.

Optimism seems a socially desirable trait in all communities. Those who share optimism are generally accepted while those who spread gloom, panic and hysteria are treated unfavorably.

In life, these people often win elections; get voted most congenial and sought for advice.

When the going gets tough, optimists get tougher

Optimists typically maintain higher levels of subjective well-being during times of stress than do people who are less optimistic. In contrast, pessimists are likely to react to stressful events by denying that they exist or by avoiding dealing with problems. Pessimists are more likely to quit trying when difficulties arise.

They persevere. They just don't give up easily,

they are also known for their patience. Inching their way a step closer to that goal or elusive dream.

Optimists are healthier and live longer

Medical research has justified that simple pleasures and a positive outlook can cause a measurable increase in the body's ability to fight disease.

Optimists' health is unusually good. They age well, much freer than most people from the usual physical ills of middle age. And they get to outlive those prone to negative thoughts. So why not be an optimist today? And think positively towards a more fulfilled life.

Why not look forward to success in all your endeavors? Why not be resilient? Like everybody else you are bound to hit lows sometimes but don't just stay there. Carry yourself out of the mud and improve your chances of getting back on the right track. And why not inspire others to remove their dark-colored glasses and see life in the bright side?

Every problem has a solution your guide to creative problem solving

More than One Way to Skin a Cat: Adventures in Creative Thinking

How many times have you caught yourself saying that there could be no other solution to a problem – and that that problem leads to a dead end? How many times have you felt stumped knowing that the problem laying before you is one you cannot solve. No leads. No options. No solutions.

Did it feel like you had exhausted all possible options and yet are still before the mountain – large, unconquerable, and impregnable? When encountering such enormous problems, you may feel like you're hammering against a steel mountain. The pressure of having to solve such a problem may be overwhelming.

But rejoice! There might be some hope yet!

With some creative problem-solving techniques you may be able to look at your problem in a different light. And that light might just be the end of the tunnel that leads to possible solutions.

First of all, in the light of creative problem-solving, you must be open-minded to the fact that there may be more than just one solution to the problem. And, you must be open to the fact that there may be solutions to problems you thought were unsolvable.

Now, with this optimistic mindset, we can try to be a little bit more creative in solving our problems.

Number one; maybe the reason we cannot solve our problems is that we have not really taken a hard look at what the problem is. Here, trying to understanding the problem and having a concrete understanding of its workings is integral solving the problem. If you know how it works, what the problem is, then you have a better foundation towards solving the problem.

Not trying to make the simple statement of what problem is. Try to identify the participating entities and what their relationships with one another are. Take note of the things you stand to gain any stand to lose from the current problem. Now you have a simple statement of what the problem is.

Number two; try to take note of all of the constraints and assumptions you have the words of problem. Sometimes it is these assumptions that obstruct our view of possible solutions. You have to identify which assumptions are valid, in which assumptions need to be addressed.

Number three; try to solve the problem by parts. Solve it going from general view towards the more detailed parts of the problem. This is called the top-down approach. Write down the question, and then come up with a one-sentence solution to that from them. The solution should be a general statement of what will solve the problem. From here you can develop the solution further, and increase its complexity little by little.

Number four; although it helps to have critical thinking aboard as you solve a problem, you must also keep a creative, analytical voice at the back of your head. When someone comes up with a prospective solution, tried to think how you could make that solution work. Try to be creative. At the same time, look for chinks in the armor of that solution.

Number five; it pays to remember that there may be more than just one solution being developed at one time. Try to keep track of all the solutions and their developments. Remember, there may be more than just one solution to the problem.

Number six; remember that old adage," two heads are better than one." That one is truer than it sounds. Always be open to new ideas. You can only benefit from listening to all the ideas each person has. This is especially true when the person you're talking to has had experience solving problems similar to yours.

You don't have to be a gung-ho, solo hero to solve the problem. If you can organize collective thought on the subject, it would be much better.

Number seven; be patient. As long as you persevere, there is always a chance that a solution will present itself. Remember that no one was able to create an invention the first time around.

Creative thinking exercises can also help you in your quest be a more creative problems solver.

Here is one example.

Take a piece of paper and write any word that comes to mind at the center. Now look at that word then write the first two words that come to your mind. This can go on until you can build a tree of related words. This helps you build analogical skills, and fortify your creative processes.

So, next time you see a problem you think you cannot solve, think again. The solution might just be staring you right in the face. All it takes is just a

little creative thinking, some planning, and a whole
lot of work.

"Cha-Lax"

Your Recommended Daily Allowance for Relaxation

Stress is the curse of living in modern times. Everyone suffers from stress. And the stress we suffer takes a heavy toll on our bodies, emotions and minds.

Feeling stressed out, worn out by fatigue or just simply having a miserable day, the best thing to do is relax.

Watching television may be a form of relaxation for some, but is not a recommended method by experts. When we watch TV we are bombarded with commercials, ads, sounds and images. So how do we achieve relaxation? If there are thousands of ways we can get stressed, one of them is not meeting deadlines, there are also many ways we can relax.

In recent studies, experts have determined that heart disease is linked to anger and irritability is linked to mental stress. Too much stress brings about ischemia that can lead to or cause a heart attack. Relaxation takes on added importance in light of this matter. Managing your anger and attitude is significant to heart health, and relaxation can help you manage stress.

One way of relaxation is transcendental meditation. Recent studies have also shown that this method might reduce artery blockage, which is a major cause for heart attack and stroke. People practice transcendental meditation by repeating uttering soothing sounds while meditating, this is to achieve total relaxation. The researchers found that practitioners of transcendental meditation significantly reduced the thickness of their arterial wall compared with those who didn't practice transcendental meditation.

Another study on another method of relaxation, acupuncture, seems to reduce high blood pressure by initiating several body functions for the brain to release chemical compounds known as endorphins. Endorphin helps to relax muscles, ease panic, decrease pain, and reduce anxiety.

Yoga is also another method for relaxation and may also have similar effects like acupuncture. In another study, participants were subjected to several minutes of mental stress. Then they were subjected to various relaxation techniques, such as listening to nature sounds or classical music. Only those who did Yoga significantly reduced the time it took for their blood pressures to go back to normal. Yoga is a form of progressive relaxation.

Breathing is one of the easiest methods to relax. Breathing influences almost all aspects of us, it affects our mind, our moods and our body. Simply focus on your breathing, after some time you can feel its effects right away.

There are several breathing techniques that can help you reduce stress.

Another easy way to achieve relaxation is exercise. If you feel irritated a simple half-hour of exercise will often settle things down. Although exercise is a great way to lose weight, it does not show you how to manage stress appropriately. Exercise should also be used in conjunction with other exercise method.

One great way of relaxation is getting a massage. To gain full relaxation, you need to totally surrender to the handling and touch of a professional therapist.

There are several types of massages that also give different levels of relaxation.

Another method of relaxation is Biofeedback. The usual biofeedback-training program includes a 10-hour sessions that is often spaced one week apart.

Hypnosis is one controversial relaxation technique. It is a good alternative for people who think that they have no idea what it feels like to be relaxed. It is also a good alternative for people with stress related health problems.

Drugs are extreme alternatives to relaxation. They are sometimes not safe and are not effective like the other relaxation methods. This method is only used by trained medical professionals on their patients.

These relaxation techniques are just some of the ways you can achieve relaxation. Another reason why we need to relax, aside from lowering blood pressure in people and decreasing the chances of a stroke or a heart attack, is because stress produces hormones that suppress the immune system, relaxation gives the immune system time to recover and in doing so function more efficiently.

Relaxation lowers the activities within the brains' limbic system; this is the emotional center of our brain.

Furthermore, the brain has a periodic need for a more pronounced activity on the right-hemisphere. Relaxation is one way of achieving this.

Relaxation can really be of good use once a relaxation technique is regularly built into your lifestyle. Choose a technique that you believe you can do regularly.

Grow spiritually a guide to spiritual development

Spiritual Growth: the Spiritual Challenge of Modern Times

To grow spiritually in a world defined by power, money, and influence is a Herculean task. Modern conveniences such as electronic equipments, gadgets, and tools as well as entertainment through television, magazines, and the web have predisposed us to confine our attention mostly to physical needs and wants. As a result, our concepts of self-worth and self-meaning are muddled. How can we strike a balance between the material and spiritual aspects of our lives?

To grow spiritually is to look inward.

Introspection goes beyond recalling the things that happened in a day, week, or month. You need to look closely and reflect on your thoughts, feelings, beliefs, and motivations. Periodically examining your experiences, the decisions you make, the relationships you have, and the things you engage in provide useful insights on your life goals, on the good traits you must sustain and the bad traits you have to discard. Moreover, it gives you clues on how to act, react, and conduct yourself in the midst of any situation. Like any skill,

127

introspection can be learned; all it takes is the courage and willingness to seek the truths that lie within you. Here are some pointers when you introspect: be objective, be forgiving of yourself, and focus on your areas for improvement.

To grow spiritually is to develop your potentials.

Religion and science have differing views on matters of the human spirit. Religion views people as spiritual beings temporarily living on Earth, while science views the spirit as just one dimension of an individual. Mastery of the self is a recurring theme in both Christian (Western) and Islamic (Eastern) teachings. The needs of the body are recognized but placed under the needs of the spirit. Beliefs, values, morality, rules, experiences, and good works provide the blueprint to ensure the growth of the spiritual being. In Psychology, realizing one's full potential is to self-actualize. Maslow identified several human needs: physiological, security, belongingness, esteem, cognitive, aesthetic, self-actualization, and self-transcendence. James earlier categorized these needs into three: material, emotional, and spiritual. When you have satisfied the basic physiological and emotional needs, spiritual or existential needs come next. Achieving each need leads to the total development of the individual. Perhaps the difference between these two religions and psychology is the end of self-development: Christianity and Islam see that self-development is a means toward serving God, while psychology view that self-development is an end by itself.

To grow spiritually is to search for meaning.

Religions that believe in the existence of God such as Christianity, Judaism, and Islam suppose that the purpose of the human life is to serve the Creator of all things. Several theories in psychology propose that we ultimately give meaning to our lives. Whether we believe that life's meaning is pre-determined or self-directed, to grow in spirit is to realize that we do not merely exist. We do not know the meaning of our lives at birth; but we gain knowledge and wisdom from our interactions with people and from our actions and reactions to the situations we are in.

As we discover this meaning, there are certain beliefs and values that we reject and affirm. Our lives have purpose. This purpose puts all our physical, emotional, and intellectual potentials into use; sustains us during trying times; and gives us something to look forward to---a goal to achieve, a destination to reach. A person without purpose or meaning is like a drifting ship at sea.

To grow spiritually is to recognize

interconnections.

Religions stress the concept of our relatedness to all creation, live and inanimate. Thus we call other people "brothers and sisters" even if there are no direct blood relations. Moreover, deity-centered religions such as Christianity and Islam speak of the relationship between humans and a higher being. On the other hand, science expounds on our link to other living things through the evolution theory.

This relatedness is clearly seen in the concept of ecology, the interaction between living and non-living things. In psychology, connectedness is a characteristic of self-transcendence, the highest human need according to Maslow. Recognizing your connection to all things makes you more humble and respectful of people, animals, plants, and things in nature. It makes you appreciate everything around you. It moves you to go beyond your comfort zone and reach out to other people, and become stewards of all other things around you.

Growth is a process thus to grow in spirit is a day-to-day encounter. We win some, we lose some, but the important thing is that we learn, and from this knowledge, further spiritual growth is made possible.

Harnessing your attraction power

Does a Law on Human Attraction Exist?

"Opposites attract" is a law of attraction, at least where electromagnetism is concerned. But are there laws about attraction between two people? "In a world that is full of strangers" as a line in a famous song of the 1980's goes, is there a clear set of rules that allows two people to fall for each other?

Is attraction a matter of chemistry?

Maybe. According to scientists, the attraction between animals of the opposite sex is all about chemicals called pheromones. The effect of pheromones in behavior of insects is the most studied to date. It has been observed, at least in some experiments, that pheromones are responsible for communication among same species and colony of ants. The horrible odor released by skunks to ward off enemies is said to be a kind of pheromone. Some species of apes rub pheromone-containing urine on the feet of potential mates to attract them. Some scientists believe that animals (usually the females) such as insects and mammals send out these chemical signals to tell the male of their species that their genes are different from theirs.

This gene diversity is important in producing offspring with better chances of survival. The perfume industry has capitalized on pheromones as a means to increase one's sexual attractiveness to the opposite sex. Animals such as the whale and the musk deer were hunted down for these chemicals.

Lately, scientists are looking into the existence of human pheromones and its role in mate selection. There are many conflicting views in the realm of biology, chemistry, genetics, and psychology. Most scientists would assert that these do not exist, or if they do, do not play a role in sexual attraction between a man and a woman. But new researches such as that conducted by Swiss researchers from the University of Bern led by Klaus Wedekind are slowly making these scientists rethink their stand. Their experiment involved women sniffing the cotton shirts of different men during their ovulation period.

It was found out that women prefer the smell of men's shirts that were genetically different, but also shared similarities with the women's genes. This, like in the case of insects and other mammals, was to ensure better and healthier characteristics for their future children. But researchers also cautioned that preference for a male odor is affected by the women's ovulation period, the food that men eat, perfumes and other scented body products, and the use of contraceptive pills.

Does personality figure in sexual attraction?

Yes, but so does your perception of a potential mate's personality. According to a research conducted by Klohnen, E.C., & S. Luo in 2003 on interpersonal attraction and personality, a person's sense of self-security and at least the person's perception of his/her partner were found to be strong determinants of attraction in hypothetical situations. What does this tell us? We prefer a certain personality type, which attracts you to a person. But aside from the actual personality of the person, which can only be verified through close interaction through time, it is your perception of your potential partner that attracts you to him/her, whether the person of your affection truly has that kind of personality or not.

This could probably account for a statement commonly heard from men and women on their failed relationships: "I thought he/she was this kind of person."

So how does attraction figure in relationships?

You have probably heard that attraction is a prelude, or a factor towards a relationship. Most probably, at least in the beginning; but attraction alone cannot make a relationship work. It is that attraction that makes you notice a person from the opposite sex, but once you get to know the person more, attraction is just one consideration. Shared values, dreams, and passions become more significant in long-term relationships.

So should I stop trying to become attractive?

More than trying to become physically attractive, work on all aspects of your health: physical, emotional, mental, and spiritual. Physical attraction is still a precursor. Remember, biology predisposes us to choose the partner with the healthiest genes. Where your emotions are concerned, just ask this to yourself: would you want to spend time with a person who feels insecure about him/herself? Probably not! There is wisdom in knowing yourself: who you are, your beliefs, values, and dreams. And do not pretend to be someone you are not.

Fooling another person by making him/her think that you share the same values and beliefs is only going to cause you both disappointments. When you are healthy in all aspects, attractiveness becomes a consequence and not an end. As mentioned in the Klohnen and Luo's research, a person's sense of self-security matters, perhaps even beyond attraction. But remember: do these things for yourself and not for other people. Only then can you truly harness your attractiveness as a person.

How to be genuinely happy

Genuine Happiness Comes from Within

Life isn't the sweetest candy. Sometimes, when I feel like the world is just too heavy, I look around and find people who continued to live fascinating and wonderful lives. And then thoughts come popping into my mind like bubbles from nowhere – "How did their life become so adorably sweet? How come they still can manage to laugh and play around despite a busy stressful life?" Then I pause and observed for awhile... I figured out that maybe, they start to work on a place called 'self'.

So, how does one become genuinely happy? Step 1 is to love yourself.

My theology professor once said that "loving means accepting." To love oneself means to accept that you are not a perfect being, but behind the imperfections must lie a great ounce of courage to be able to discover ways on how to improve your repertoire to recover from our mistakes.

Genuine happiness also pertains to contentment. When you are contented with the job you have, the way you look, with your family, your friends, the place you live in, your car, and all the things you now have – truly, you know the answer to the question "how to be genuinely happy."

When we discover a small start somewhere from within, that small start will eventually lead to something else, and to something else. But if you keep questioning life lit it has never done you any good, you will never be able to find genuine happiness.

I believe that life is about finding out about right and wrong, trying and failing, winning and losing. These are things that happen as often as you inhale and exhale. Failure, in a person's life has become as abundant and necessary as air. But this should not hinder us from becoming happy.

How to be genuinely happy in spite all these? I tell you... every time you exert effort to improve the quality of life and your being, whether it is cleaning up your room, helping a friend, taking care of your sick dog, fail on board exams and trying again, life gives you equivalent points for that.

Imagine life as a big score board like those which are used in the NFLs. Every time you take a step forward, you make scoring points. Wouldn't it be nice to look at that board at the end of each game and think to yourself "Whew! I got a point today. I'm glad I gave it a shot.", instead of looking at it all blank and murmur "Geez, I didn't even hit a score today. I wish I had the guts to try out. We could have won!" and then walk away.

Genuine happiness isn't about driving the hottest Formula 1 car, nor getting the employee of the year award, earning the highest 13th month pay, or beating the sales quota. Sometimes, the most sought after prizes in life doesn't always go to the fastest, the strongest, the bravest or not even the best. So, how do you become genuinely happy? Everyone has his own definition of 'happiness'.

Happiness for a writer may mean launching as much bestselling books as possible. Happiness for a basketball rookie may mean getting the rookie of the year award. Happiness for a beggar may mean a lot of money. Happiness for a business man may mean success. So, really now, how do we become genuinely happy? Simple. You don't have to have the best things in this world. It's about doing and making the best out of every single thing. When you find yourself smiling at your own mistake and telling yourself "Oh, I'll do better next time", you carry with you a flame of strong will power to persevere that may spread out like a brush fire. You possess a willingness to stand up again and try – that will make you a genuinely happy person.

When you learn to accept yourself and your own faults. You pass step 1 in the project "how to become genuinely happy". For as long as you know how to accept others, you will also be accepted. For as long as you love and know how to love, you will receive love ten folds back.

Again, throw me that same question "how to become genuinely happy?". I'll refer you to a friend of mine who strongly quoted- "Most of us know that laughter is the best medicine to life's aches and pain. But most of us don't know that the best kind of laughter is laughter over self. Coz then you don't just become happy... you become free."

It's time to start a Healthy life

"The Way to Wellness" It's time to start a Healthy life: your 7 days program

How many times have you gone to sleep at night, swearing you'll go to the gym in the morning, and then changing your mind just eight hours later because when you get up, you don't feel like exercising?

While this can happen to the best of us, it doesn't mean you should drop the ball altogether when it comes to staying fit. What people need to realize is that staying active and eating right are critical for long-term health and wellness -- and that an ounce of prevention is worth a pound of cure. The more you know about how your body responds to your lifestyle choices, the better you can customize a nutrition and exercise plan that is right for you. When you eat well, increase your level of physical activity, and exercise at the proper intensity, you are informing your body that you want to burn a substantial amount of fuel. This translates to burning fat more efficiently for energy. In other words, proper eating habits plus exercise equals fast metabolism, which, in turn gives you more energy throughout the day and allows you to do more physical work with less effort.

The true purpose of exercise is to send a repetitive message to the body asking for improvement in metabolism, strength, aerobic capacity and overall fitness and health. Each time you exercise, your body responds by upgrading its capabilities to burn fat throughout the day and night, Exercise doesn't have to be intense to work for you, but it does need to be consistent.

I recommend engaging in regular cardiovascular exercise four times per week for 20 to 30 minutes per session, and resistance training four times per week for 20 to 25 minutes per session. This balanced approach provides a one-two punch, incorporating aerobic exercise to burn fat and deliver more oxygen, and resistance training to increase lean body mass and burn more calories around the block.

Here's a sample exercise program that may work for you:

* Warm Up -- seven to eight minutes of light aerobic activity intended to increase blood flow and lubricate and warm-up your tendons and joints.

* Resistance Training -- Train all major muscle groups. One to two sets of each exercise. Rest 45 seconds between sets.

* Aerobic Exercise -- Pick two favorite activities, they could be jogging, rowing, biking or cross-country skiing, whatever fits your lifestyle. Perform 12 to 15 minutes of the first activity and continue with 10 minutes of the second activity. Cool down during the last five minutes.

* Stretching -- Wrap up your exercise session by stretching, breathing deeply, relaxing and meditating.

When starting an exercise program, it is important to have realistic expectations. Depending on your initial fitness level, you should expect the following changes early on.

* From one to eight weeks -- Feel better and have more energy.

* From two to six months -- Lose size and inches while becoming leaner. Clothes begin to fit more loosely. You are gaining muscle and losing fat.

* After six months -- Start losing weight quite rapidly.

Once you make the commitment to exercise several times a week, don't stop there. You should also change your diet and/or eating habits,' says Zwiefel. Counting calories or calculating grams and percentages for certain nutrients is impractical. Instead, I suggest these easy-to-follow guidelines:

* Eat several small meals (optimally four) and a couple of small snacks throughout the day
* Make sure every meal is balanced -- incorporate palm-sized proteins like lean meats, fish, egg whites and dairy products, fist-sized portions of complex carbohydrates like whole-wheat bread and pasta, wild rice, multigrain cereal and potatoes, and fist-sized portions of vegetable and fruits
* Limit your fat intake to only what's necessary for adequate flavor
* Drink at least eight 8-oz. glasses of water throughout the day
* I also recommend that you take a multi-vitamin each day to ensure you are getting all the vitamins and minerals your body needs.

I suppose that's all I can think of for now. I should extend my thanks to a doctor friend of mine. Without him, I wouldn't be able to write this article, or keep my sanity.

Enjoy life, we all deserve it.

Make it happen be a leader

How to Become an Ideal Leader

When you are at work, do you get frustrated because things don't seem to be happening the way they're supposed to be? You see people milling around but nothing gets accomplished. And in the daily hustle and bustle, do you feel that your goals remain just that – goals. Then maybe it's time for you to stand up and do something about it.

Most people are content just to stand around listening for orders. And it isn't unusual to adopt a follow-the-leader mentality. But maybe, somewhere inside of you, you feel the desire to make things happen – to be the head, not the tail. Then maybe leadership just suits you fine.

Some people believe that great leaders are made, not born. Yes, it may be true that some people are born with natural talents. However, without practice, without drive, without enthusiasm, and without experience, there can be no true development in leadership.

You must also remember that good leaders are continually working and studying to improve their natural skills. This takes a commitment to constantly improve in whatever endeavor a person chooses.

First of all, let's define leadership. To be a leader, one must be able to influence others to accomplish a goal, or an objective. He contributes to the organization and cohesion of a group.

Contrary to what most people believe, leadership is not about power. It is not about harassing people or driving them using fear. It is about encouraging others towards the goal of the organization. It is putting everyone on the same page and helping them see the big picture of the organization. You must be a leader not a boss.

First of all, you have to get people to follow you. How is this accomplished?

People follow others when they see a clear sense of purpose. People will only follow you if they see that you know where you are going. Remember that bumper sticker? The one that says, don't follow me, I'm lost too? The same holds true for leadership. If you yourself do not know where you're headed to, chances are people will not follow you at all.

You yourself must know the vision of the organization. Having a clear sense of hierarchy, knowing who the bosses are, who to talk to, the organization's goals and objectives, and how the organization works is the only way to show others you know what you are doing.

Being a leader is not about what you make others do. It's about who you are, what you know, and what you do. You are a reflection of what you're subordinates must be.

Studies have shown that one other bases of good leadership is the trust and confidence your subordinates have of you. If they trust you they will go through hell and high water for you and for the organization.

Trust and confidence is built on good relationships, trustworthiness, and high ethics.

The way you deal with your people, and the relationships you build will lay the foundation for the strength of your group. The stronger your relationship, the stronger their trust and confidence is in your capabilities.

Once you have their trust and confidence, you may now proceed to communicate the goals and objectives you are to undertake.

Communication is a very important key to good leadership. Without this you cannot be a good leader. The knowledge and technical expertise you have must be clearly imparted to other people.

Also, you cannot be a good leader and unless you have good judgment. You must be able to assess situations, weigh the pros and cons of any decision, and actively seek out a solution.

It is this judgment that your subordinates will come to rely upon. Therefore, good decision-making is vital to the success of your organization.

Leaders are not do-it-all heroes. You should not claim to know everything, and you should not rely upon your skills alone.

You should recognize and take advantage of the skills and talents your subordinates have. Only when you come to this realization will you be able to work as one cohesive unit.

Remember being a leader takes a good deal of work and time. It is not learned overnight. Remember, also, that it is not about just you. It is about you and the people around you.

So, do you have the drive and the desire to serve required of leaders? Do you have the desire to work cooperatively with other people? Then start now. Take your stand and be leader today.

Meditation techniques

Do Yoda Proud: Meditation 101

Meditation refers to a state where your body and mind are consciously relaxed and focused. Practitioners of this art report increased awareness, focus, and concentration, as well as a more positive outlook in life.

Meditation is most commonly associated with monks, mystics and other spiritual disciplines. However, you don't have to be a monk or mystic to enjoy its benefits. And you don't even have to be in a special place to practice it. You could even try it in your own living room!

Although there are many different approaches to meditation, the fundamental principles remain the same. The most important among these principles is that of removing obstructive, negative, and wandering thoughts and fantasies, and calming the mind with a deep sense of focus. This clears the mind of debris and prepares it for a higher quality of activity.

The negative thoughts you have – those of noisy neighbors, bossy officemates, that parking ticket you got, and unwanted spam– are said to contribute to the 'polluting' of the mind, and shutting them out is allows for the 'cleansing' of the mind so that it may focus on deeper, more meaningful thoughts.

Some practitioners even shut out all sensory input – no sights, no sounds, and nothing to touch – and try to detach themselves from the commotion around them. You may now focus on a deep, profound thought if this is your goal. It may seem deafening at first, since we are all too accustomed to constantly hearing and seeing things, but as you continue this exercise you will find yourself becoming more aware of everything around you.

If you find the meditating positions you see on television threatening – those with impossibly arched backs, and painful-looking contortions – you need not worry. The principle here is to be in a comfortable position conducive to concentration. This may be while sitting cross-legged, standing, lying down, and even walking.

If the position allows you to relax and focus, then that would be a good starting point. While sitting or standing, the back should be straight, but not tense or tight. In other positions, the only no-no is slouching and falling asleep.

Loose, comfortable clothes help a lot in the process since tight fitting clothes have a tendency to choke you up and make you feel tense.

The place you perform meditation should have a soothing atmosphere. It may be in your living room, or bedroom, or any place that you feel comfortable in. You might want an exercise mat if you plan to take on the more challenging positions (if you feel more focused doing so, and if the contortionist in you is screaming for release). You may want to have the place arranged so that it is soothing to your senses.

Silence helps most people relax and meditate, so you may want a quiet, isolated area far from the ringing of the phone or the humming of the washing machine. Pleasing scents also help in that regard, so stocking up on aromatic candles isn't such a bad idea either.

The monks you see on television making those monotonous sounds are actually performing their mantra. This, in simple terms, is a short creed, a simple sound which, for these practitioners, holds a mystic value.

You do not need to perform such; however, it would pay to note that focusing on repeated actions such as breathing, and humming help the practitioner enter a higher state of consciousness.

The principle here is focus. You could also try focusing on a certain object or thought, or even, while keeping your eyes open, focus on a single sight.

One sample routine would be to – while in a meditative state – silently name every part of your body and focusing your consciousness on that part. While doing this you should be aware of any tension on any part of your body. Mentally visualize releasing this tension. It works wonders.

In all, meditation is a relatively risk-free practice and its benefits are well worth the effort (or non-effort – remember we're relaxing).

Studies have shown that meditation does bring about beneficial physiologic effects to the body. And there has been a growing consensus in the medical community to further study the effects of such. So in the near future, who knows, that mystical, esoteric thing we call meditation might become a science itself!

Motivation the heart of self improvement

Pain may sometimes be the reason why people change. Getting flunked grades make us realize that we need to study. Debts remind us of our inability to look for a source of income. Being humiliated gives us the 'push' to speak up and fight for ourselves to save our face from the next embarrassments. It may be a bitter experience, a friend's tragic story, a great movie, or an inspiring book that will help us get up and get just the right amount of motivation we need in order to improve ourselves.

With the countless negativities the world brings about, how do we keep motivated? Try on the tips I prepared from A to Z...

A - Achieve your dreams. Avoid negative people, things and places. Eleanor Roosevelt once said, "the future belongs to those who believe in the beauty of their dreams."

B - Believe in yourself, and in what you can do.

C – Consider things on every angle and aspect. Motivation comes from determination. To be able to understand life, you should feel the sun from both sides.

D – Don't give up and don't give in. Thomas Edison failed once, twice, more than thrice before he came up with his invention and perfected the incandescent light bulb. Make motivation as your steering wheel.

E – Enjoy. Work as if you don't need money. Dance as if nobody's watching. Love as if you never cried. Learn as if you'll live forever. Motivation takes place when people are happy.

F – Family and Friends – are life's greatest 'F' treasures. Don't lose sight of them.

G – Give more than what is enough. Where does motivation and self improvement take place at work? At home? At school? When you exert extra effort in doing things.

H – Hang on to your dreams. They may dangle in there for a moment, but these little stars will be your driving force.

I – Ignore those who try to destroy you. Don't let other people to get the best of you. Stay out of toxic people – the kind of friends who hates to hear about your success.

J – Just be yourself. The key to success is to be

yourself. And the key to failure is to try to please everyone.

K – keep trying no matter how hard life may seem. When a person is motivated, eventually he sees a harsh life finally clearing out, paving the way to self improvement.
L – Learn to love yourself. Now isn't that easy?

M – Make things happen. Motivation is when your dreams are put into work clothes.

N – Never lie, cheat or steal. Always play a fair game.

O – Open your eyes. People should learn the horse attitude and horse sense. They see things in 2 ways – how they want things to be, and how they should be.

P – Practice makes perfect. Practice is about motivation. It lets us learn repertoire and ways on how can we recover from our mistakes.

Q – Quitters never win. And winners never quit. So, choose your fate – are you going to be a quitter? Or a winner?

R – Ready yourself. Motivation is also about preparation. We must hear the little voice within us telling us to get started before others will get on their feet and try to push us around. Remember, it wasn't raining when Noah build the ark.

S – Stop procrastinating.

T – Take control of your life. Discipline or self control jives synonymously with motivation. Both are key factors in self improvement.

U – Understand others. If you know very well how to talk, you should also learn how to listen. Yearn to understand first, and to be understood the second.

V – Visualize it. Motivation without vision is like a boat on a dry land.

W – Want it more than anything. Dreaming means believing. And to believe is something that is rooted out from the roots of motivation and self improvement.

X – X Factor is what will make you different from the others. When you are motivated, you tend to put on "extras" on your life like extra time for family, extra help at work, extra care for friends, and so on.

Y – You are unique. No one in this world looks, acts, or talks like you. Value your life and existence, because you're just going to spend it once.

Z – Zero in on your dreams and go for it!!!

Positive attitude can change the world around you

The Powers of a Positive Attitude

I am going to ask you to something very weird right now. First of all, I want you to listen to your thoughts. Now tell me, what thoughts fill your head? Would you label them as positive, or negative?

Now let's say you are walking down the street with these thoughts. Do you think anyone who would meet you would be able to tell you what's on your mind?

The answer to number one is up to you. But, the answer number two can be pretty generic. Although people will not be able to tell you exactly what you think, they will more or less have an idea of how you are feeling.

Here's another question. When you enter a party filled with friends, do they all fall silent as if something terrible had happened? Or does everybody there perk up as if waiting for something exciting to happen?

You know what? The answer to all these depends on your frame of mind.

Thoughts are very powerful. They affect your general attitude. The attitude you carry reflects on your appearance, too – unless, of course, you are a great actor.

And it doesn't end there. Your attitude can also affect people around you.

The type of attitude you carry depends on you. It can be either positive or negative.

Positive thoughts have a filling effect. They are admittedly invigorating. Plus, the people around the person carrying positive thoughts are usually energized by this type of attitude.

Negative thoughts on the other hand have a sapping effect on other people. Aside from making you look gloomy and sad, negative thoughts can turn a festive gathering into a funeral wake.

A positive attitude attracts people, while a negative attitude repels them. People tend to shy away from those who carry a negative attitude.

We can also define attitude as the way of looking at the world. If you choose to focus on the negative things in the world, more or less you have a negative attitude brewing up. However, if you choose to focus on the positive things, you are more likely carry a positive attitude.

You have much to gain from a very positive attitude. For one, studies have shown that a positive attitude promotes better health. Those with this kind of attitude also have more friends. projecting a positive attitude also helps one to handle stress and problems better than those who have a negative attitude.

A positive attitude begins with a healthy self-image. If you will love the way you are and are satisfied, confident, and self-assured, you also make others are around feel the same way.

A negative attitude, on the other hand, has, of course, an opposite effect. So, carrying a negative attitude has a twofold drawback. You feel bad about yourself, and you make others feel the same way.

If you want to have a positive attitude, you have to feature healthy thoughts. This is probably very hard to do nowadays since, all around us, the media feeds us nothing but negative thoughts. A study shows that for every 14 things a parent says to his or her child, only one is positive. This is truly a saddening thought.

If you want a healthier outlook in life, you need

to think happy thoughts, and you have to hear positive things as well. So, what can you do? Well, for starters, you could see a funny movie, you could play with children, spend some time telling jokes with friends. All these activities fill you with positive stimuli, which in turn promotes positive attitude.

Although it is impossible to keep ourselves from the negative things around us, you can still carry a positive attitude by focusing on the good things, the positive things in life.

And this positive attitude you now carry can be of benefit to other people. Sometimes when other people feel down, the thing people mostly do is try to give them advice. But sometimes, all they need is somebody to sit by them, and listen to them. If you have a positive attitude you may be able to cheer them up without even having to say anything.

If positive attitude is really great, why do people choose to adopt a negative attitude instead? One who carries a negative attitude may be actually sending a signal for attention. Before you get me wrong, feeling sad, angry, or gloomy is not wrong itself. But dwelling on these thoughts for far too long is not healthy either. There is a time to mourn.

As always, if you are beset by troubles, even in

your darkest hour, focus on the good things in life, you will always have hope. Problems become something you can overcome.

You do not have much to lose by adopting a healthy, positive attitude. Studies show that such an attitude actually retards aging, makes you healthier, helps you develop a better stress coping mechanism, and has a very positive effect on all the people you meet every day. So, what's not to like about a positive attitude? Adopt one today.

Self empowerment using people unlock your social potential

Power through the people

Have you come across a person who is so naturally friendly that when you put him inside a room of strangers, he'll be friends with almost everyone in no time? We call such a people-person, someone unbelievably nice and charismatic that he can charm anyone into doing anything.

A socially-empowered person achieves so much greatness, basically because of the people that catapult him to success. He earns the trust and all-out support of the people, whom he had helped before. He never runs out of help. He can do anything with the plethora of people behind him. All because he knows he maximizes his social potential!

See, if you know your social skills and you make use of them, you will reach self-empowerment. Self-empowerment is making a general overhaul in your life and turning yourself into a happier and more successful person. If you can be one of those people-persons, then I can't see any reason why you will not succeed. You just have to know how to start.

1. Be genuine.

Hypocrisy will just bring you all the way down. Be genuinely nice and interested to people. Once they perceive that you are Mr. Hypocrite with selfish intentions, you might as well say goodbye to self-empowerment.

2. Be the greatest listener that you can be.

To earn the love and trust of the people, listen to their problems and sympathize with them. Do not just hear them out, listen to them with your heart. Make eye contact when the person talks to you. Listen as if every word matters, and it does. Brownie points when they find out that there is a confidante in you.

3. Laugh out loud.

I do not mean that you force yourself to laugh for every joke cracked by someone, albeit you do not find it funny at all. This means finding humor in things and not being too darn serious. A person oozing with an awesome sense of humor attracts crowds and eventually, attracts success.

4. Don't forget yourself.

In the process of fluttering around like a social butterfly, you might forget yourself, allowing everyone to push you over. Remember, love and value yourself before anyone else. If you deem yourself respectable and worthy of affection, people will flock to you and not trample on you.

5. Do random acts of kindness.

You don't have to do a John Rockefeller and blow your savings to charity. Little acts of kindness matters the most, and this can be as simple as giving someone a surprise you-take-care card or helping an elderly cross the street. When we were kindergarten students, kindness was taught to us and greatly practiced. Now is the time to revive the good deeds and this time, let them stay for good.

6. Contact your old friends.

Sad how some friendships are destined to goodbye, but thanks to technology, you can do something about it. Relive the good old days by flipping your yearbook and look for the great people whom you want to communicate with again. Adding these old friends to your roster of support peers will surely make you feel good all over.

7. Develop your personality.

Are you grouchy, grumpy and generally morose? Whoa, you can't go through life with those. Get rid of the bad traits and habits that perpetually hamper your growth. And really, who wants a grouchy friend anyway?

8. Be confident.

Be able to stride to the other corner of the room and introduce yourself to people with that winning smile of yours. Just remember: be confident, not arrogant.

9. Practice control.

When angry, don't snap at anyone. Never throw a tantrum. Stay calm and collected. Be adult enough to take control of situation and transform your anger into something more productive and passive. As soon as people think your anger goes to volcanic proportions easily, they will find it hard to come to you.

10. Keep nurturing your relationships.

Your relationship with your family, friends and significant others is too precious that you must not neglect it whatever happens. Go out and have fun with them. Do things together. Happiness will never fly from your side as long as the people who matter the most are close to you. In the end, using people for self-empowerment means becoming a better and more lovable person. It's a win-win situation: the people know they can turn to you anytime and vice versa.

Self improvement and success

Everything that happens to us happens in purpose. And sometimes, one thing leads to another. Instead of locking yourself up in your cage of fears and crying over past heartaches, embarrassment and failures, treat them as your teachers and they will become your tools in both self improvement and success.

I remember watching Patch Adams – it's my favorite movie, actually. It's one great film that will help you improve yourself. Hunter "patch" Adams is a medical student who failed to make it through the board exams. After months of suffering in melancholy, depression and suicidal attempts – he decided to seek for medical attention and voluntarily admitted himself in a psychiatric ward. His months of stay in the hospital led him to meeting different kinds of people. Sick people in that matter. He met a catatonic, a mentally retarded, a schizophrenic and so on.

Patch found ways of treating his own ailment and finally realized he has to get back on track. He woke up one morning realizing that after all the failure and pains he has gone through, he still want to become the a doctor. He carries with himself a positive attitude that brought himself improvement and success. He didn't only improved himself, but also the life of the people around him and the quality of life. Did he succeed? Needless to say, he became the best damn doctor his country has ever known.

So, when does self improvement become synonymous with success? Where do we start? Take these tips, friends...
*Stop thinking and feeling as if you're a failure, because you're not. How can others accept you if YOU can't accept YOU?

*When you see hunks and models on TV, think more on self improvement, not self pitying. Self acceptance is not just about having nice slender legs, or great abs. Concentrate on inner beauty.

*When people feel so down and low about themselves, help them move up. Don't go down with them. They'll pull you down further and both of you will end up feeling inferior.

*The world is a large room for lessons, not mistakes. Don't feel stupid and doomed forever just because you failed on a science quiz. There's always a next time. Make rooms for self improvement.

*Take things one at a time. You don't expect black sheep's to be goody-two-shoes in just a snap of a finger. Self improvement is a one day at a time process.

*Self improvement results to inner stability, personality development and dig this …. SUCCESS. It comes from self confidence, self appreciation and self esteem.

* Set meaningful and achievable goals. Self improvement doesn't turn you to be the exact replica of Cameron Diaz or Ralph Fiennes. It hopes and aims to result to an improved and better YOU.

*Little things mean BIG to other people. Sometimes, we don't realize that the little things that we do like a pat on the back, saying "hi" or "hello", greeting someone "good day" or telling Mr. Smith something like "hey, I love your tie!" are simple things that mean so much to other people. When we're being appreciative about beautiful things around us and other people, we also become beautiful to them.

*When you're willing to accept change and go through the process of self improvement, it doesn't mean that everyone else is. The world is a place where people of different values and attitude hang out. Sometimes, even if you think you and your best friend always like to do the same thing together at the same time, she would most likely decline an invitation for self improvement.

We should always remember that there's no such thing as 'overnight success'. It's always a wonderful feeling to hold on to the things that you already have now, realizing that those are just one of the things you once wished for. A very nice quote says that "When the student is ready, the teacher will appear." We are all here to learn our lessons. Our parents, school teachers, friends, colleagues, officemates, neighbors... they are our teachers. When we open our doors for self improvement, we increase our chances to head to the road of success.

Start your own coaching

"The Game of Life" Start your own coaching: 7 days program

Have you ever been a coach to a neighborhood team? I know how it feels the first time I've coached a team of seven-year-old soccer kids and how much they can really test my patience, not to mention sanity as they run around kicking the ball like ants to a huge, white crumb. It feels strange at first, having to be stared at by a bunch of kids who they will know that I'm not the one in the field. Sounds wrong in a sense, right? But what is the dead about coaching?

Coaching is all about being a, well, 'coach' in the corporate world of handlers, front-liners and even a couple of benchwarmers biding their time to be given a chance to perform. I know how that feels when I go back to my regular day job. Some players are just MVP material, and some of them are just to support the MVP's so why bother sticking around? It sounds ironic when they say 'there is no I in team', but even the underachievers can be sore losers as well.

These are steps that can be done within the day, and no matter what, it takes determination to be a coach.

1. There is a WHOLE lot of talk these days about Corporate Team Building. There are many, many options: vacation packages, rope courses, on-going office games, ice-breakers, etc. Management can also purchase videos, books, and seminar packages to assist them in building up their organization into a team worthy of belonging. A little later I will give you some ideas of where you can go for information on these team-building tools.

2. The truth about motivation is waiting to be grasped! It is ripe and ready for you to put into action today. Don't settle for mind-numbing gibberish. Get practical in 3 small ways to begin looking forward to your alarm clock sounding off each morning before you huddle with the team.

3. Experience is the best thing despite of what course you graduated in. There is something about being a people person who knows how to stir the energetic side of one individual, and more so when you mix it up with an entire team.

4. To question a person by his or her performance is sometimes required, but never question their knowledge or their intelligence. Sadly, I have seen a few mistakes from past coaches who never seem to understand what a player has to go through to get the job right. It will lead to further aggravation and maybe even hostility. If you want the job done right, then go do it yourself. You'll see how it is to be at the receiving end and it will help your set a much better course for improvement.

5. Sending a player to the bench is probably the worse experience a coach has to go through, especially if your player is the top performer. In dealing with this kind of person, see to it that he spills his guts voluntarily. Egotism in a performer tends to make them lose their focus on even the smallest mistakes, then you can catch him or her red handed. Be firm, but understanding about it.

6. Don't allow your position to blind you from what you are supposed to do. Even coaches are human enough to think that they are far more superior, but only by rank. Even if you have been in their shoes when you were their age, it's better to dole out a piece of wisdom in order for them to realize that this will be for their own benefit.

7. Lastly, you should learn to trust yourself and your team. Decisions and performance are primarily your goals, and there are many of them to see if they could perform the task much more efficiently. So before you think about sending one member to the bench, have a good chat with him or her and see if they have any problems. If it's too personal, then just encourage them to do their best and it also helps to give them a good, encouraging slap on the back.

I guess there's all there is to it. Being a corporate drone myself, I know how important it is for a company to be successful, and we're all part of that success. Coaches are there not to make your work a little difficult just because you have either an attitude problem or not much a performer, but they're the guides who will help you perform as hard as you can possibly can. You'll do them proud one of these days, as well as you.

Take decision live your own life

Life is About Choices
and the Decisions We Make

Life is like a road. There are long and short roads; smooth and rocky roads; crooked and straight paths. In our life many roads would come our way as we journey through life. There are roads that lead to a life of single blessedness, marriage, and religious vocation. There are also roads that lead to fame and fortune on one hand, or isolation and poverty on the other. There are roads to happiness as there are roads to sadness, roads towards victory and jubilation, and roads leading to defeat and disappointment.

Just like any road, there are corners, detours, and crossroads in life. Perhaps the most perplexing road that you would encounter is a crossroad. With four roads to choose from and with limited knowledge on where they would go, which road will you take? What is the guarantee that we would choose the right one along the way? Would you take any road, or just stay where you are: in front of a crossroad?

There are no guarantees.

You do not really know where a road will lead you

until you take it. There are no guarantees. This is one of the most important things you need to realize about life. Nobody said that choosing to do the right thing all the time would always lead you to happiness. Loving someone with all your heart does not guarantee that it would be returned. Gaining fame and fortune does not guarantee happiness. Accepting a good word from an influential superior to cut your trip short up the career ladder is not always bad, especially if you are highly qualified and competent. There are too many possible outcomes, which your really cannot control. The only thing you have power over is the decisions that you will make, and how you would act and react to different situations.

Wrong decisions are always at hindsight.

Had you known that you were making a wrong decision, would you have gone along with it? Perhaps not, why would you choose a certain path when you know it would get you lost? Why make a certain decision if you knew from the very beginning that it is not the right one. It is only after you have made a decision and reflected on it that you realize its soundness. If the consequences or outcomes are good for you, then you have decided correctly. Otherwise, your decision was wrong.

Achieve what you can believe

Take the risk: decide.

Since life offers no guarantee and you would never know that your decision would be wrong until you have made it, then you might as well take the risk and decide. It is definitely better than keeping yourself in limbo. Although it is true that one wrong turn could get you lost, it could also be that such a turn could be an opportunity for an adventure, moreover open more roads. It is all a matter of perspective. You have the choice between being a lost traveler or an accidental tourist of life. But take caution that you do not make decisions haphazardly. Taking risks is not about being careless and stupid. Here are some pointers that could help you choose the best option in the face of life's crossroads:

· **Get as many information as you can about your situation.**

You cannot find the confidence to decide when you know so little about what you are faced with. Just like any news reporter, ask the 5 W's: what, who, when, where, and why. What is the situation? Who are the people involved? When did this happen? Where is this leading? Why are you in this situation? These are just some of the possible questions to ask to know more about your situation. This is important. Oftentimes, the reason for indecision is the lack of information about a situation.

- **Identify and create options.**

What options do the situation give you? Sometimes the options are few, but sometimes they are numerous. But what do you do when you think that the situation offers no options? This is the time that you create your own. Make your creative mind work. From the most simplistic to the most complicated, entertain all ideas. Do not shoot anything down when an idea comes to your head. Sometimes the most outrageous idea could prove to be the right one in the end. You can ask a friend to help you identify options and even make more options if you encounter some difficulty, but make sure that you make the decision yourself in the end.

- **Weigh the pros and cons of every option.**

Assess each option by looking at the advantages and disadvantages it offers you. In this way, you get more insights about the consequences of such an option.

- **Trust yourself and make that decision.**

Now that you have assessed your options, it is now time to trust yourself. Remember that there are no guarantees and wrong decisions are always at hindsight. So choose... decide... believe that you are choosing the best option at this point in time.

Now that you have made a decision, be ready to face its consequences: good and bad. It may take you to a place of promise or to a land of problems. But the important thing is that you have chosen to live your life instead of remaining a bystander or a passive audience to your own life. Whether it is the right decision or not, only time can tell. But do not regret it whatever the outcome. Instead, learn from it and remember that you always have the chance to make better decisions in the future.

The basics of goal settings

Setting Your Goals - Easier Said, Easily Done

The basics of setting a goal is an open secret known by top-caliber athletes, successful businessmen and businesswomen and all types of achievers in all the different fields. The basics of setting goals give you short-term and long-term motivation and focus. They help you set focus on the acquisition of required knowledge and help you to plan and organize your resources and your time so that you can get the best out of your life.

Setting clearly defined short term and long term goals will enable you to measure your progress and achieve personal satisfaction once you have successfully met your goals. Charting your progress will also enable you to actually see the stages of completion leading to the actual realization of your goals. This eliminates the feeling of a long and pointless grind towards achieving your goal. Your self-confidence and level of competence will also improve as you will be more aware of your capabilities as you complete or achieve your goals.

The basics of goal settings will involve deciding what you really want to do with your personal life and what short term and long term goals you need to achieve it. Then you have to break down goals into the smaller and manageable targets that you must complete in your way to achieving your lifetime targets. Once you have your list waste no time in tackling your goals.

A good way to have a manageable list is to have a daily and weekly set of goals. By doing this you will be always in the position of going towards you life plan goals. Everyday will give you the opportunity to fulfill a certain goal giving you the feeling of accomplishment.

Here are some pointers that should be taken into consideration in setting goals and achieving them.

Attitude plays a very big role in setting and achieving your goals. You must ask yourself if any part of you or your mind holding you back towards completing your simplest goals? If there are any part of your behavior that is being a hindrance or puts your plans into disarray? If you do have problems in these areas then the immediate thing to do is to address this problem. Solutions may include a visit to a doctor or psychiatrist to control your emotions.

Careers are made by good time management practice. Failing in a career is often attributed to bad time management. Careers require a lot from an individual which often makes the career the life of the individual. Plan how far do you want to go into your career.

Education is key in achieving your goals. If your goals require you to have a certain kind of degree or require a certain specialization or demand a certain skill to be developed, make plans in getting the appropriate education.

Your family should never be left out of your plans. If you are just starting out then you have to decide if you want to be a parent or when you want to be a parent. You also have to know if you really would be a good parent and how well would you relate to extended family members

Personal financial situations also play a major role in achieving your goals. Have a realistic goal on how much you really want to earn. You also must be able to create plans or stages by which you will be able to reach your earning potential.

Physically gifted individuals may be able to achieve sports related goals like being in the National Basketball association or National Football League. Determining your physical capabilities should be one of your priorities. Physical limitations could however be conquered with proper planning.

As the saying goes -'All work and no play makes Jack a dull boy', or something to that effect, is by all means true down to the last the letter. Giving yourself a little pleasure: should be included into your plans.

The power of relationships

Creating Effective and Efficient Relationships

Relationships of all kinds are often perceived as very delicate things, that require extra effort to maintain. However, a relationship can also be something that can provide security and can also be long lasting despite many trials.

Building an effective and lasting relationships is a necessity for several reasons. For example in a group or organization, the well being of the people depends on how efficient and effective that group or organization works.

The group or organization is also dependent on how the members work well with the management.

An ineffective group or organization can really be very frustrating. An effective group or organization can also ask so much on their members, that sometimes the members would be having no life outside the walls of the area where they work or sacrifice the other aspects of their life just to meet deadlines. For an organization or group with this kind of scenario, relationships can be stressed or suffer from breakdown.

People or other entities who depend on these groups or organization also suffer.

Society is defined as a web of relationships, which requires all parties to work and contribute their share in order to achieve a common goal. Having a relationship that is good, where cooperation and respect are manifested, can make society work better. In this way each member works for the good of the whole and towards achieving a common goal. This can only be attained with effective and efficient relationships.

Understanding the other parties' feeling and position creates an effective and efficient relationship. The easiest method to understand what is important to another party is to ask them what they want and listen to what they have to say. When the other party realizes this, they would feel the importance given to them

Effective and efficient relationships require parties to openly express their feelings and positions on all matters pertinent on the relationship. Assuming that the other party understands our needs and give us when we need it without asking for it is not a good practice.

Respect is the key to relationship. In order to create a more effective relationship, parties should treat each other with respect. We can show respect just by listening to the other party and by trying sincerely to understand how they function. You can also show respect to other parties by confirming that they are doing everything they can.

The opposite of respect is quick forming of judgments based on unfounded facts and prejudice.

Respect is the very foundation for a great relationship. This also means respecting yourself and respecting others.

Another key area in forming an effective relationship is to tackle differences of the other party directly. Differences between parties or people are quite interesting. For example in a conversation where each party listens to the other party, you may observe that each is having two different perspectives.

Work towards a win-win solution for both parties.

This can be done when at least one party acknowledges that the relationship is important. That party would then exert more time, effort and energy to understand the other party's needs and deal with it to get it out of the way. Should they fail, it is comforting for that party to know that they tried.

Effectively listening and no pre-judging. This is important if parties are to understand each other.

Informal discussions are conducive for parties. They bring out issues and concerns comfortably. They also feel more relaxed making them think more clearly.

Developing an atmosphere where the other party can express their feelings when they need to.

When parties fail to express whatever is on their mind or their feelings, it can get in the way of building an effective relationship.

Parties should be aware that certain things exist naturally but should be controlled in any dealings in any relationship. Human nature is one. Some of these things found in a relationship also include a history of stereotyping or mistrust, blaming the other person or party for a strained relationship, excluding the other party's feelings when focusing on a task, no clear and defined objectives, roles and expectations of each party in a relationship is also unclear.

Relationships are important to anyone, addressing issues and problems right away is a must to further improve the relationship. As they say 'No man is an Island'.

Unleash your creative thinking

Creative Notions

People seem to have the misconception that only a select few are able to unleash a steady flow of creative genius. That is not true at all. The fact is, creativity is very much like a muscle that needs to be exercised in order to consistently give out great results. If you don't practice harnessing creative thinking, this skill will very much atrophy into inexistence. But keep working and this skill will soon come to you in a snap.

So how do you unleash your creative thinking? Well, the first thing is to become a human leech. No, we're not talking about just sucking the blood out of every living being available, we're saying that you should take in as much knowledge and learning you can find. Read everything available -- good and bad, and keep your mind open to the infinite possibilities of the universe. The more you know, the more you'll want to know, and the more your faculty of wonder will be exercised. Prepare to be amazed at little facts that add a bit of color into your life.

Focus on a creative activity every day. Yes, it's an effort. Even doodling is a creative activity. Don't let anything hinder you. Mindlessness may be a creative activity, but for people who are just

189

starting out to unleash a little bit of creative thinking in their lives, it is helpful and encouraging to have concrete evidence, that, "hey, what I'm doing is getting somewhere." So why don't you try it. Practice drawing for a couple of minutes each day. Bring out your old camera and start snapping photos like crazy. Keep a journal and make a point to write in it religiously. Another cool idea is to write by describing something with your five senses.

Try to avoid vague adjectives like "marvelous," "amazing," and "delicious." Before you know it, you'll have built yourself a tiny portfolio, and you'll be amazed at the growth you've undertaken after amassing all those works of art. Who knows, you might actually take to liking those things you do every day. Pretty soon those things will become a part of you and you'll be addicted to these creative exercises.

Think out of the box -- or don't. Sometimes, constraints are actually a good thing. Limitations discipline you to work within your means. It enables you to be more resourceful. Creative freedom is great, but limitations enforce discipline.

Try something new every day and let your experiences broaden your perspective. Explore a new district in your neighborhood. Spend an afternoon in a museum to which you've never been before. Chat up someone on the bus. Open up to the people around you. As you thrust yourself out of your comfort zone more and more each day, your sense of adventure grows and so does your zest for life. Think about it. When was the last time you did something for the first time? If it's been a while, I tell you, you've been missing out on a whole lot of experiences that could've added to your growth, emotionally, mentally, physically, or spiritually. Why don't you try bungee jumping today? Not only will you learn, but you will also have plenty of stories to share, enabling you to practice your storytelling skills and making you the life of the party.

Embrace insanity. No, not to the point of practically admitting yourself into the mental ward. As John Russell once said, "Sanity calms, but madness is more interesting." Exactly! Every creative thought was once deemed insanity by other "normal" people at one time or another. Luckily, that didn't stop the creative geniuses from standing by them. The thing is, sanity or being normal confines people to think... well, normally. Within limits. Creativity is essentially breaking through barriers. Yes, this includes the bizarre and the downright strange. I'm not saying that you yourself should develop a creative personality.

That might go haywire. An example of a

creative personality would be George Washington, who often rode into battle naked, or James Joyce, who wrote "Dubliners" with beetle juice for an intense fear of ink, or Albert Einstein, who thought his cat was a spy sent by his rival (or in thinking creatively in this case, the term could probably be "arch nemesis.") It's important that your creativity doesn't get you detached from the real world completely.

I hope this article has inspired you to start thinking beyond your "limits." If you follow these steps pretty soon you'll be living a life full of interesting adventures. Unleashing your creative thinking will bring about a new zest for living life.

Unlock yourself improvement power

UNLOCK YOUR SELF IMPROVEMENT POWER

When we look at a certain object, a painting for example – we won't be able to appreciate what's in it, what is painted and what else goes with it if the painting is just an inch away from our face. But if we try to take it a little further, we'll have a clearer vision of the whole art work.

We reach a point in our life when we are ready for change and a whole bunch of information that will help us unlock our self improvement power. Until then, something can be staring us right under our nose but we don't see it. The only time we think of unlocking our self improvement power is when everything got worst. Take the frog principle for example –

Try placing Frog A in a pot of boiling water. What happens? He twerps! He jumps off! Why? Because he is not able to tolerate sudden change in his environment – the water's temperature. Then try Frog B: place him in luke warm water, then turn the gas stove on. Wait till the water reaches a certain boiling point. Frog B then thinks "Ooh... it's a bit warm in here".

People are like Frog B in general. Today, Anna thinks Carl hates her. Tomorrow, Patrick walks up to her and told her he hates her. Anna stays the same and doesn't mind her what her friends says. The next day, she learned that Kim and John also abhors her. Anna doesn't realize at once the importance and the need for self improvement until the entire community hates her.

We learn our lessons when we experience pain. We finally see the warning signs and signals when things get rough and tough. When do we realize that we need to change diets? When none of our jeans and shirts would fit us. When do we stop eating candies and chocolates? When all of our teeth has fallen off. When do we realize that we need to stop smoking? When our lungs have gone bad. When do we pray and ask for help? When we realize that we're going to die tomorrow.

The only time most of us ever learn about unlocking our self improvement power is when the whole world is crashing and falling apart. We think and feel this way because it is not easy to change. But change becomes more painful when we ignore it.

Change will happen, like it or hate it. At one point or another, we are all going to experience different turning points in our life – and we are all going to eventually unlock our self improvement power not because the world says so, not because our friends are nagging us, but because we realized it for our own good.

Happy people don't just accept change, they embrace it. Now, you don't have to feel a tremendous heat before realizing the need for self improvement. Unlocking yourself improvement power means unlocking yourself up in the cage of thought that "it is just the way I am". It is such a poor excuse for people who fear and resist change. Most of us program our minds like computers.

Jen repeatedly tells everyone that she doesn't have the guts to be around groups of people. She heard her mom, her dad, her sister, her teacher tell the same things about her to other people. Over the years, that is what Jen believes. She believes it's her story. And what happens? Every time a great crowd would troop over their house, in school, and in the community – she tends to step back, shy away and lock herself up in a room. Jen didn't only believed in her story, she lived it.

Jen has to realize that she is not what she is in her story. Instead of having her story post around her face for everyone to remember, she has to have the spirit and show people "I am an important person and I should be treated accordingly!"

Self improvement may not be everybody's favorite word, but if we look at things in a different point of view, we might have greater chances of enjoying the whole process instead of counting the days until we are fully improved. Three sessions in a week at the gym would result to a healthier life, reading books instead of looking at porn will shape up a more profound knowledge, going out with friends and peers will help you take a step back from work and unwind. And just when you are enjoying the whole process of unlocking yourself improvement power, you'll realize that you're beginning to take things light and become happy.

What can time management bring to your personal growth

The Key to a Better Life

Time management is basically about being focused. The Pareto Principle also known as the '80:20 Rule' states that 80% of efforts that are not time managed or unfocused generates only 20% of the desired output. However, 80% of the desired output can be generated using only 20% of a well time managed effort. Although the ratio '80:20' is only arbitrary, it is used to put emphasis on how much is lost or how much can be gained with time management.

Some people view time management as a list of rules that involves scheduling of appointments, goal settings, thorough planning, creating things to do lists and prioritizing. These are the core basics of time management that should be understood to develop an efficient personal time management skill. These basic skills can be fine tuned further to include the finer points of each skill that can give you that extra reserve to make the results you desire.

But there is more skills involved in time management than the core basics. Skills such as decision making, inherent abilities such as emotional intelligence and critical thinking are also essential to your personal growth.

Personal time management involves everything you do. No matter how big and no matter how small, everything counts. Each new knowledge you acquire, each new advice you consider, each new skill you develop should be taken into consideration.

Having a balanced life-style should be the key result in having personal time management. This is the main aspect that many practitioners of personal time management fail to grasp.

Time management is about getting results, not about being busy.

The six areas that personal time management seeks to improve in anyone's life are physical, intellectual, social, career, emotional and spiritual.

The physical aspect involves having a healthy body, less stress and fatigue.

The intellectual aspect involves learning and other mental growth activities.

The social aspect involves developing personal

or intimate relations and being an active contributor to society.

The career aspect involves school and work.

The emotional aspect involves appropriate feelings and desires and manifesting them.

The spiritual aspect involves a personal quest for meaning.

Thoroughly planning and having a set of things to do list for each of the key areas may not be very practical, but determining which area in your life is not being giving enough attention is part of time management. Each area creates the whole you, if you are ignoring one area then you are ignoring an important part of yourself.

Personal time management should not be so daunting a task. It is a very sensible and reasonable approach in solving problems big or small.

A great way of learning time management and improving your personal life is to follow several basic activities.

One of them is to review your goals whether it be immediate or long-term goals often.

A way to do this is to keep a list that is always accessible to you.

Always determine which task is necessary or not necessary in achieving your goals and which activities are helping you maintain a balanced life style.

Each and every one of us has a peek time and a time when we slow down, these are our natural cycles. We should be able to tell when to do the difficult tasks when we are the sharpest.

Learning to say "No". You actually see this advice often. Heed it even if it involves saying the word to family or friends.

Pat yourself at the back or just reward yourself in any manner for an effective time management result.

Try and get the cooperation from people around you who are actually benefiting from your efforts of time management.

Don't procrastinate. Attend to necessary things immediately.

Have a positive attitude and set yourself up for success. But be realistic in your approach in achieving your goals.

Have a record or journal of all your activities. This will help you get things in their proper perspective.

These are the few steps you initially take in becoming a well rounded individual.

As the say personal time management is the art and science of building a better life.

From the moment you integrate into your life time management skills, you have opened several options that can provide a broad spectrum of solutions to your personal growth. It also creates more doors for opportunities to knock on.

What you should know about Leadership

Leadership Exposed: Things You Thought You Knew About Leadership

Much has been written about leadership: rules, pointers, styles, and biographies of inspiring leaders throughout world history. But there are certain leadership ideas that we ourselves fail to recognize and realize in the course of reading books. Here is a short list of things you thought you knew about leadership.

1. Leaders come in different flavors.

There are different types of leaders and you will probably encounter more than one type in your lifetime. Formal leaders are those we elect into positions or offices such as the senators, congressmen, and presidents of the local clubs. Informal leaders or those we look up to by virtue of their wisdom and experience such as in the case of the elders of a tribe, or our grandparents; or by virtue of their expertise and contribution on a given field such as Albert Einstein in the field of Theoretical Physics and Leonardo da Vinci in the field of the Arts. Both formal and informal leaders

practice a combination of leadership styles.
· Lewin's three basic leadership styles – authoritative, participative, and delegative
· Likert's four leadership styles – exploitive authoritative, benevolent authoritative, consultative, and participative
· Goleman's six emotional leadership styles - visionary, coaching, facilitative, democratic, pacesetting, and commanding.

2. Leadership is a process of becoming.

Although certain people seem to be born with innate leadership qualities, without the right environment and exposure, they may fail to develop their full potential. So like learning how to ride a bicycle, you can also learn how to become a leader and hone your leadership abilities. Knowledge on leadership theories and skills may be formally gained by enrolling in leadership seminars, workshops, and conferences. Daily interactions with people provide the opportunity to observe and practice leadership theories.

Together, formal and informal learning will help you gain leadership attitudes, gain leadership insights, and thus furthering the cycle of learning. You do not become a leader in one day and just stop. Life-long learning is important in becoming a good leader for each day brings new experiences that put your knowledge, skills, and attitude to a test.

3. Leadership starts with you.

The best way to develop leadership qualities is to apply it to your own life. As an adage goes "action speaks louder than words." Leaders are always in the limelight. Keep in mind that your credibility as a leader depends much on your actions: your interaction with your family, friends, and co-workers; your way of managing your personal and organizational responsibilities; and even the way you talk with the newspaper vendor across the street. Repeated actions become habits. Habits in turn form a person's character. Steven Covey's book entitled 7 Habits of Highly Effective People provides good insights on how you can achieve personal leadership.

4. Leadership is shared.

Leadership is not the sole responsibility of one person, but rather a shared responsibility among members of an emerging team. A leader belongs to a group. Each member has responsibilities to fulfill. Formal leadership positions are merely added responsibilities aside from their responsibilities as members of the team. Effective leadership requires members to do their share of work. Starting as a mere group of individuals, members and leaders work towards the formation of an effective team. In this light, social interaction plays a major role in leadership.

To learn how to work together requires a great deal of trust between and among leaders and members of an emerging team. Trust is built upon actions and not merely on words. When mutual respect exists, trust is fostered and confidence is built.

5. Leadership styles depend on the situation.

How come dictatorship works for Singapore but not in the United States of America? Aside from culture, beliefs, value system, and form of government, the current situation of a nation also affects the leadership styles used by its formal leaders. There is no rule that only one style can be used. Most of the time, leaders employ a combination of leadership styles depending on the situation. In emergency situations such as periods of war and calamity, decision-making is a matter of life and death. Thus, a nation's leader cannot afford to consult with all departments to arrive at crucial decisions.

The case is of course different in times of peace and order---different sectors and other branches of government can freely interact and participate in governance. Another case in point is in leading organizations. When the staffs are highly motivated and competent, a combination of high delegative and moderate participative styles of leadership is most appropriate. But if the staffs have low competence and low commitment, a combination of high coaching, high supporting, and high directing behavior from organizational leaders is required.

Now that you are reminded of these things, keep in mind that there are always ideas that we think we already know; concepts we take for granted, but are actually the most useful insights on leadership.

Why is it important to improve yourself

WHY IS IT IMPORTANT TO IMPROVE YOUR SELF?

Sometimes, when all our doubts, fears and insecurities wrap ourselves up, we always come up with the idea of "I wish I was somebody else." More often than not, we think and believe that someone or rather, most people are better than us.- when in reality, the fact is, most people are more scared than us.

You spot a totally eye-catching girl sitting by herself at a party, casually sipping on a glass of Asti Spumoni. You think to yourself, "she looks so perfectly calm and confident." But if you could read thru her transparent mind, you would see a bunch of clouds of thoughts and you might just be amazed that she's thinking "are people talking about why I am seated here alone?... Why don't guys find me attractive? ...I don't like my ankles, they look too skinny... I wish I was as intelligent as my best friend."

We look at a young business entrepreneur and say "Woo... what else could he ask for?" He stares at himself at the mirror and murmur to himself, "I hate my big eyes... I wonder why my friends won't talk to me... I hope mom and dad would still work things out."

Isn't it funny? We look at other people, envy them for looking so outrageously perfect and wish we could trade places with them, while they look at us and thinks of the same thing. We are insecure of other people who themselves are insecure of us. We suffer from low self-esteem, lack of self-confidence and lose hope in self improvement because we are enveloped in quiet desperation.

Sometimes, you notice that you have an irritating habit like biting off your finger nails, having a foul mouth, and you – of all people, is the last to know.

I have a friend who never gets tired of talking. And in most conversations, she is the only one who seems to be interested in the things she has to say. So all of our other friends tend to avoid the circles whenever she's around, and she doesn't notices how badly she became socially handicapped – gradually affecting the people in her environment.

One key to self improvement is to LISTEN and TALK to a trusted friend. Find someone who you find comfort in opening up with even the most gentle topics you want to discuss. Ask questions like "do you think I am ill-mannered?", "Do I always sound so argumentative?", "Do I talk too loud?", "Does my breath smell?", "Do I ever bore you when were together?". In this way, the other person will obviously know that you are interested in the process of self improvement. Lend her your ears for comments and criticisms and don't give her answers like "Don't exaggerate! That's just the way I am!" Open up your mind and heart as well. And in return, you may want to help your friend with constructive criticism that will also help her improve herself.

One of Whitney Houston's songs says "Learning to love yourself is the greatest love of all." True enough. In order to love others, you must love yourself too. Remember, you cannot give what you do not have.

Before telling other people some ways on how to improve themselves, let them see that you yourself is a representation and a product of self improvement. Self improvement makes us better people, we then inspire other people, and then the rest of the world will follow.

Stop thinking of yourselves as second-rate beings. Forget the repetitive thought of "If only I was richer... if only I was thinner" and so on. Accepting your true self is the first step to self improvement. We need to stop comparing ourselves to others only to find out at the end that we've got

10 more reasons to envy them.

We all have our insecurities. Nobody is perfect. We always wish we had better things, better features, better body parts, etc. But life need not to be perfect for people to be happy about themselves. Self improvement and loving yourself is not a matter of shouting to the whole world that you are perfect and you are the best. It's the virtue of acceptance and contentment. When we begin to improve ourselves, we then begin to feel contented and happy.

Your 5 minute daily program to Stress management

"Relaxing with a Mental PDA" Your 5 minutes daily program to Stress management

We all have this favorite expression when it comes to being stressed out, and I wouldn't bother naming all of them since it may also vary in different languages. But when it comes down to it, I think that it is how we work or even relax, for that matter that triggers stress. Ever been stressed even when you're well relaxed and bored? I know I have.

Since Error! Hyperlink reference not valid. is unavoidable in life, it is important to find ways to decrease and prevent stressful incidents and decrease negative reactions to stress. Here are some of the things that can be done by just remembering it, since life is basically a routine to follow like brushing your teeth or eating breakfast. You can do a few of them in a longer span of time, but as they say-- every minute counts.

Managing time

Time management skills can allow you more time with your family and friends and possibly increase your performance and productivity. This will help reduce your stress.

To improve your time management:

· Save time by focusing and concentrating, delegating, and scheduling time for yourself.
· Keep a record of how you spend your time, including work, family, and leisure time.
· Prioritize your time by rating tasks by importance and urgency. Redirect your time to those activities that are important and meaningful to you.
· Manage your commitments by not over- or under committing. Don't commit to what is not important to you.
· Deal with procrastination by using a day planner, breaking large projects into smaller ones, and setting short-term deadlines.
· Examine your beliefs to reduce conflict between what you believe and what your life is like.
Build healthy coping strategies

It is important that you identify your coping strategies. One way to do this is by recording the stressful event, your reaction, and how you cope in a stress journal. With this information, you can work to change unhealthy coping strategies into healthy ones-those that help you focus on the positive and what you can change or control in your life.

Lifestyle

Some behaviors and lifestyle choices affect your stress level. They may not cause stress directly, but they can interfere with the ways your body seeks relief from stress. Try to:

· Balance personal, work, and family needs and obligations.
· Have a sense of purpose in life.
· Get enough sleep, since your body recovers from the stresses of the day while you are sleeping.
· Eat a balanced diet for a nutritional defense against stress.
· Get moderate exercise throughout the week.
· Limit your consumption of alcohol.
· Don't smoke.

Social support

Social support is a major factor in how we experience stress. Social support is the positive support you receive from family, friends, and the community. It is the knowledge that you are cared for, loved, esteemed, and valued. More and more research indicates a strong relationship between social support and better mental and physical health.

Changing thinking

When an event triggers negative thoughts, you may experience fear, insecurity, anxiety, depression, rage, guilt, and a sense of worthlessness or powerlessness. These emotions trigger the body's stress, just as an actual threat does. Dealing with your negative thoughts and how you see things can help reduce stress.

· Thought-stopping helps you stop a negative thought to help eliminate stress.
· Disproving irrational thoughts helps you to avoid exaggerating the negative thought, anticipating the worst, and interpreting an event incorrectly.
· Problem solving helps you identify all aspects of a stressful event and find ways to deal with it.
· Changing your communication style helps you communicate in a way that makes your views known without making others feel put down, hostile, or intimidated. This reduces the stress that comes from poor communication. Use the assertiveness ladder to improve your communication style.

Even writers like me can get stressed even though we're just using our hands to do the talking, but having to sit for 7 or 8 hours is already stressful enough and have our own way to relieve stress. Whether you're the mail guy, the CEO, or probably the average working parent, stress is one unwanted visitor you would love to boot out of your homes, especially your life.

Your 7 days program to Positive thinking

I'm sure you have a bright idea hidden somewhere in the back of your mind that you just can't wait to test out. Of course you're not the only one with the bright idea. So what motivates you to churn those creative, or even inspiring juices to its utmost flavor?

It's always best to set up a personal goal where you can accomplish the most in record time, maybe like mowing the lawn in an hour before the big game on TV. A correct and positive attitude in whatever you do will make things easier, and even enjoyable.

Here are some tips to make it through the week even if you're just sitting in your favorite couch. An idea takes time to form in your head and is always at work while you are busy sitting.

Having a bit of positive thinking can help you realize things that are never thought possible. Thinking big is indeed the American Way and that what made our country prosperous.

1. Take passionate action towards living your life by design. Talk is cheap. Action = deposits in the bank of a passionately authentic future. Without

215

it, passion is void.

This is a perfect example where dreams are made of where you start by tinkering with your mind, then with your hands. And if the idea weakens, you can always go back to it later until you finish it.

2. Commit to yourself as well as those you love to create powerfully a life you can love. Instead of reacting, commit to creating from your heart and soul, out of love rather than fear. The American Dream will always be there, but a dream will still be a dream without motion. Be amazed as the transformation begins.

3. Recognize and embrace the thought that each moment is perfect regardless of its outcome. Every time you hit on something that may appear too extreme, why not give it a shot and see if it will work. You will be surprised to see if there are other ways to get the task done in time. If you are not pleased with the outcome, decide to use that moment to learn from and make the appropriate shift.

4. Dwell completely in a place of gratitude. Learn to utilize what you have in your hands and make use of it in the most constructive way. Slipping into neediness will become less of a habit when you repeatedly shift towards gratitude, away from poverty consciousness.

5. Use a Passion Formula of Recognize/Reevaluate/Restore in place of the Should a/Would a/Could a whirlwind. The former is based in increased knowledge and abundance while the latter focuses on scarcity and lack. As you face people or tasks that may seem harder than scaling the summit of the Himalayas, allow yourself to realize that the task is just as important as giving out orders to your subordinates. You would rather be richly passionate!

6. Keep humor at the forefront of thought, laughing at and with yourself when possible. You may find yourself quite entertaining when you loosen up! I am yet to see a comedian ever go hungry even though his jokes are as 'old as great-grandma'. Life has so much to offer to allow you to mope around in self pity. Humor is very attractive, very passionate: life-giving.

7. Believe that you are the architect of your destiny. No one can take your passionate future from you except for you! Create your life authentically. As long as there's still breath in your body, there is no end to how much you can accomplish in a lifetime. The concept of thinking big is all about enjoying your work, which would lead to celebrate a discovery that is born within your hands. Watch everything flow into place with perfect, passionate precision.

It's interesting how people get swallowed up by something trivial as learning to use a computer, when nowadays that top computer companies are manufacturing software that even the kids can do it. I don't mean to be condescending, but that's the idea of not having any positive thinking in your life-you'll just end up as a dim bulb in a dark corner. So instead of subjecting yourself to what you will be doomed for, make your path by taking the first step with a positive attitude.

Your 7 days program to self improvement

"A Better You" Your 7 days program to self-improvement

I seem to lost count on how many times I've read and heard of celebrity marriages failing almost left and right. Not that I care (and personally I don't), it seems strange that we often see movie and TV stars as flawless people, living the fairytale life of riches and glamour. I suppose we all have to stop sticking our heads in the clouds and face reality.

There are many ways to lose your sense of self-esteem despite of how trivial it could get. But whatever happens, we should all try not to lose our own sense of self.

So what does it take to be a cut above the rest? Here are some of the things you can think and improve on that should be enough for a week.

1. Know your purpose
Are you wandering through life with little direction - hoping that you'll find happiness, health and prosperity? Identify your life purpose or mission statement and you will have your own unique compass that will lead you to your truth north every

time.

This may seem tricky at first when you see yourself to be in a tight or even dead end. But there's always that little loophole to turn things around and you can make a big difference to yourself.

2. Know your values
What do you value most? Make a list of your top 5 values. Some examples are security, freedom, family, spiritual development, learning. As you set your goals for 2005 - check your goals against your values. If the goal doesn't align with any of your top five values - you may want to reconsider it or revise it.

The number shouldn't discourage you, instead it should motivate you to do more than you can ever dreamed of.

3. Know your needs
Unmet needs can keep you from living authentically. Take care of yourself. Do you have a need to be acknowledged, to be right, to be in control, to be loved? There are so many people who lived their lives without realizing their dreams and most of them end up being stressed or even depressed for that matter. List your top four needs and get them met before it's too late!

4. Know your passions

You know who you are and what you truly enjoy in life. Obstacles like doubt and lack of enthusiasm will only hinder you, but will not derail your chance to become the person you ought to be. Express yourself and honor the people who has inspired you to become the very person you wanted to be.

5. Live from the inside out

Increase your awareness of your inner wisdom by regularly reflecting in silence. Commune with nature. Breathe deeply to quiet your distracted mind. For most of us city slickers it's hard to even find the peace and quiet we want even in our own home. In my case I often just sit in a dimly lit room and play some classical music. There's sound, yes, but music does soothe the savage beast.

6. Honor your strengths

What are your positive traits? What special talents do you have? List three - if you get stuck, ask those closest to you to help identify these. Are you imaginative, witty, good with your hands? Find ways to express your authentic self through your strengths. You can increase your self-confidence when you can share what you know to others.

7. Serve others

When you live authentically, you may find that you develop an interconnected sense of being. When you are true to who you are, living your purpose and giving of your talents to the world around you, you give back in service what you came to share with others -your spirit - your essence. The rewards for sharing your gift with those close to you is indeed rewarding, much more if it were to be the eyes of a stranger who can appreciate what you have done to them.

Self-improvement is indeed one type of work that is worth it. It shouldn't always be within the confines of an office building, or maybe in the four corners of your own room. The difference lies within ourselves and how much we want to change for the better.

Your 7 days program to Stress management

"Have One Week, Will Relax" Your 7 days program to Stress management

They say there's more than one way to skin a cat. The same goes when you start tearing your hair out with all the frustration, grief, anxiety, and yes, stress. It's a state of mental conditioning that is like taking that bitter pill down your throat, causing you to lose your sense of self, and worse your sanity. Just thinking about it can drive anyone off the edge.

And they say that the proactive ones are already living off the edge.

As one stressed-out person to another, I know how it feels, and believe me there are many variants when it comes to stress. Coping with life, and carrying the problems that may or may not belong to you can scratch away the little joy and happiness that you can carry once you head out that door. You can't blame them for being like that; they have their own reasons, so much like we have our reasons to allow stress to weigh us down. They say that stress is all in the mind, well, what's bugging you anyway?

There are several ways to manage stress, and eventually remove it out of your life one of these days. So I'll try to divide it into a seven-day course for you and I promise it's not going to be too taxing on the body, as well as on the mind.

1. Acknowledge that some stress is good
Make stress your friend! Based on the body's natural "fight or flight" response, that burst of energy will enhance your performance at the right moment. I've yet to see a top sportsman totally relaxed before a big competition. Use stress wisely to push yourself that little bit harder when it counts most.

2. Avoid stress sneezers
Stressed people sneeze stress germs indiscriminately and before you know it, you are infected too!

Protect yourself by recognizing stress in others and limiting your contact with them. Or if you've got the inclination, play stress doctor and teach them how to better manage themselves.

3. Learn from the best
When people around are losing their head, who keeps calm? What are they doing differently? What is their attitude? What language do they use? Are they trained and experienced?

Figure it out from afar or sit them down for a chat. Learn from the best stress managers and copy what they do.

4. Practice socially acceptable heavy breathing
This is something I've learned from a gym instructor: You can trick your body into relaxing by using heavy breathing. Breathe in slowly for a count of 7 then breathe out for a count of 11. Repeat the 7-11 breathing until your heart rate slows down, your sweaty palms dry off and things start to feel more normal.

5. Give stress thoughts the red light
It is possible to tangle yourself up in a stress knot all by yourself. "If this happens, then that might happen and then we're all up the creek!" Most of these things never happen, so why waste all that energy worrying needlessly?

Give stress thought-trains the red light and stop them in their tracks. Okay so it might go wrong - how likely is that, and what can you do to prevent it?

6. Know your trigger points and hot spots
Presentations, interviews, meetings, giving difficult feedback, tight deadlines.... My heart rate is cranking up just writing these down!

Make your own list of stress trigger points or hot

spots. Be specific. Is it only presentations to a certain audience that get you worked up? Does one project cause more stress than another? Did you drink too much coffee?

Knowing what causes you stress is powerful information, as you can take action to make it less stressful. Do you need to learn some new skills? Do you need extra resources? Do you need to switch to decaf?

7. Burn the candle at one end
Lack of sleep, poor diet and no exercise wreaks havoc on our body and mind. Kind of obvious, but worth mentioning as it's often ignored as a stress management technique. Listen to your mother and don't burn the candle at both ends!

So having stress can be a total drag, but that should not hinder us to find the inner peace of mind that we have wanted for a long time. In any case, one could always go to the Bahamas and bask under the summer sun.

Your secret to success have a vision of who you are and want to be

Life Mapping: A Vision of Success

Success is more than economic gains, titles, and degrees. Planning for success is about mapping out all the aspects of your life. Similar to a map, you need to define the following details: origin, destination, vehicle, backpack, landmarks, and route.

Origin: Who you are

A map has a starting point. Your origin is who you are right now. Most people when asked to introduce themselves would say, "Hi, I'm Jean and I am a 17-year old, senior high school student." It does not tell you about who Jean is; it only tells you her present preoccupation. To gain insights about yourself, you need to look closely at your beliefs, values, and principles aside from your economic, professional, cultural, and civil status. Moreover, you can also reflect on your experiences to give you insights on your good and not-so-good traits, skills, knowledge, strengths, and weaknesses. Upon introspection, Jean realized that she was highly motivated, generous, service-oriented, but impatient. Her inclination was in the biological-medical field. Furthermore, she believed that life must serve a purpose, and that wars were destructive to human dignity.

Destination: A vision of who you want to be

"Who do want to be?" this is your vision. Now it is important that you know yourself so that you would have a clearer idea of who you want to be; and the things you want to change whether they are attitudes, habits, or points of view. If you hardly know yourself, then your vision and targets for the future would also be unclear. Your destination should cover all the aspects of your being: the physical, emotional, intellectual, and spiritual. Continuing Jean's story, after she defined her beliefs, values, and principles in life, she decided that she wanted to have a life dedicated in serving her fellowmen.

Vehicle: Your Mission

A vehicle is the means by which you can reach your destination. It can be analogized to your mission or vocation in life. To a great extent, your mission would depend on what you know about yourself. Bases on Jean's self-assessment, she decided that she was suited to become a doctor, and that she wanted to become one. Her chosen vocation was a medical doctor. Describing her vision-mission fully: it was to live a life dedicated to serving her fellowmen as a doctor in conflict-areas.

Travel Bag: Your knowledge, skills, and attitude

Food, drinks, medicines, and other travelling necessities are contained in a bag. Applying this concept to your life map, you also bring with you certain knowledge, skills, and attitudes. These determine your competence and help you in attaining your vision. Given such, there is a need for you to assess what knowledge, skills, and attitudes you have at present and what you need to gain along the way. This two-fold assessment will give you insights on your landmarks or measures of success. Jean realized that she needed to gain professional knowledge and skills on medicine so that she could become a doctor. She knew that she was a bit impatient with people so she realized that this was something she wanted to change.

Landmarks and Route: S.M.A.R.T. objectives

Landmarks confirm if you are on the right track while the route determines the travel time. Thus, in planning out your life, you also need to have landmarks and a route. These landmarks are your measures of success. These measures must be specific, measurable, attainable, realistic, and time bound. Thus you cannot set two major landmarks such as earning a master's degree and a doctorate degree within a period of three years, since the minimum number of years to complete a master's degree is two years. Going back to Jean as an example, she identified the following landmarks in her life map: completing a bachelor's degree in biology by the age of 21; completing medicine by the age of 27; earning her specialization in infectious diseases by the age of 30; getting deployed in local public hospitals of their town by the age of 32; and serving as doctor in war-torn areas by the age of 35.

Anticipate Turns, Detours, and Potholes

The purpose of your life map is to minimize hasty and spur-of-the-moment decisions that can make you lose your way. But oftentimes our plans are modified along the way due to some inconveniences, delays, and other situations beyond our control. Like in any path, there are turns, detours, and potholes thus; we must anticipate them and adjust accordingly.

Key Questions That Set You Apart

Am I a sponge for discovery and opportunity?
Do I devour information that keeps me sharp to the current events that affect my markets?

Am I a true optimist?
Do I think of problems as opportunities?

Am I forward-looking?
Am I satisfied with the status quo?

Am I a risk-taker?
Do I usually act on my hunches?

Do I have passion?
Do I stick to my efforts instead of quitting? Do I love what I do?

Am I competitive?
Do I think in competitive terms to motivate me?

Am I money wise?
Do I understand costs and values?

Was I an entrepreneur at a young age?
Did I have the entrepreneurial spirit early on?

Am I time conscious?
Do I know the value of time and how to use it?

Am I overtly curious?
Do I ask a lot of questions about how things work?

Am I a solitary worker?
Do I work best by myself or on a team?

Am I professional at all times?
Am I easily distracted by outside influences?

Do I have high energy?
Do I maintain myself, my well-being and my mental stability?

7-Level Success Seminars™
Mind Your Business Seminars™
Mark Zupo Seminars™

...Reserve your seat NOW!

"MAKE YOUR BUSINESS YOUR LIFE AND MAKE YOUR LIFE YOUR BUSINESS!"

\-   **MARK ZUPO**

Opportunity Pages

Don't Spend Years Trying to Write Your Book!

There is a Fast and Painless Way to Write a Book Without Having to Actually Write it Word For Word!

The Secrets to Writing & Selling Your First Book Fast!

The Original How to "Write and Sell Your First Book" Workshop

You have always thought of writing a book and you know that you just can't find the time, right? Now you can...because I will show you how; to do it faster than you ever thought possible!

The **"YourFastBook™"** Workshop will give you all the tools you'll ever need to "blast" out a book in no time flat!

In the "YourFastBook™" workshop, you'll learn:

- How to write your book without ever putting pen to paper!

- How to market your book without ever paying a publisher!
- How to make you book available to millions with a click of a button!
- How to avoid the 10 most common mistakes authors make!
- How to protect your with this simple free technique!
- How to never pay a royalty and keep all the profit for yourself!

Still Not Convinced?

I am the author or co-author of more-than 23 books to date. I am a "best-selling" author and credible authority on the self-publishing secrets that the conventional industry publishers don't want to you to know.

Check this out! When you enroll in my award-winning workshop you'll get all this and more;

- How to write your book in one day!
- How to give your book and award-winning title!
- The three secrets to every author's success with future orders!
- How to turn your book into a "Money-Machine"
- How to make people pay five times what you paid for printing!

- Why the best books never get published and are lost forever!
- How to develop multiple streams of income from your book

You MUST get in on this workshop right NOW!

Classes fill up quickly, so <u>sign-up now and become a self-published author</u>!

Workshop Details:

Become an author and wow your friends and relatives. Start your book now by enrolling in this exclusive workshop today!

Follow Mark on: Twitter and Facebook for insight, inspiration, and motivation with words of wisdom, encouragement and enthusiasm!

Choose the One-on-One Book *eConference* Package with Mark Zupo.

Here is the format for the Executive Author Conference:

- **eConference 1** We will nail down the focus of your book, the title and niche market wants and needs, idea and synopsis. Then we'll devise a plan for writing, printing, marketing and self-publishing it. We will tailor your personal objectives and timeline for completion of the book content. I will give you some of the resources for the writing, printing, publishing you will need at this stage.

- **eConference 2** Here we will evaluate the content of your book, formulate questions and answers that will deliver the materials that will become chapters. We'll talk about the process of establishing a brand, finding a market, positioning your book for discovery and methods of future income from your book.

- **eConference 3** In this session we bring together the content, the format and completeness of the book. We discuss income streams and methods for future books. At this stage we can start to see the results of the book in real life.

Note*   We will schedule three 1-hour, one-on-one conferences (via Freeconferencecall.com, iChat, Skype or Telephone). Also, there will be 2-3 additional hours of discussion via email to unite your work with the industry standard for what a book must contain.

This purpose of this package is to focus your idea and material into a print-ready product to begin your life as a self-published author. This package is not for people who sit around and talk about how hard it is to write a book!

This package is proven method of self-publishing. This is your opportunity to be a self-published author with lightning speed!

All resources, tools and materials provided. Audio conversation recordings provided at additional cost. Tele-Seminars with other authors, expert authors and industry experts are included.

SCHEDULE **YOURFASTBOOK™ Executive eConference** now!

Mark Zupo

Send to:

YourFastBook.com

1-678-640-0585 09:00 – 5:00 EST

www.7LevelSuccess.com

Mark's Books;

1. "You Deserve to be Rich"

The Secrets to Earning What You're Really Worth

2. From Mess to Millionaire

One Man's Story of Failure to Success

3. 7-Level Success Millionaire®

Move From Ordinary to Extraordinary Success in Life & Business

4. "You're Not The Boss Of Me"

The Secrets to Empowering Today's Youth to Independence and   Success

5. Money Mouth - Speak for Yourself

The 7-Secrets of How to Make You're Living Speaking

6. How I DIDN'T climb Mt. Everest

And 23 other non- events that didn't shape my life

8. Dean of the DUMP!

Life secrets I learned when I lived at the garbage dump!

Sources and Resources

Mark's speaking career in industry spans 25 years. He has delivered more-than, 1,200 presentations. From his experiences he has authored and co-authored many books on self development, business development techniques and marketing enterprises. Mark speaks on several topics that enlighten, entertain and motivate his audiences to action!

Mark Zupo is a dynamic and insightful speaking talent, recognized for his empowering and motivational focus to your success. As a driven leader with a Commanding Presence, he Motivates, Inspires, Energizes and Empowers his audience.

Mark Zupo has been the driving force in changing the lives of anyone within range of his voice. Mark's "3-Foot Rule" makes him one of the most sought-after speakers in his industry. Find the topic or topics that are a sure fit to you and your organization and schedule Mark to speak at your event soon.

To find out more about Mark and his other activities,

please visit us at: www.MarkZupo.com

Mark's Most Requested Topics/Programs:

- <u>The Adversity University</u>

  "Build Power, Credibility and Respect from Life's Lessons"

- <u>7-Secrets of Business Success</u>

  "The Keys to Wealth and Freedom"

- <u>Leadership</u>

  "From Ability to Credibility"

Schedule Mark to Speak at Your Next Event!

Contact us:

1-678-640-0585 09:00 – 5:00 EST

Mark Zupo International, LLC

Sources and Resources

Mark's speaking career in industry spans 25 years. He has delivered more-than, 1,200 presentations. From his experiences he has authored and co-authored many books on self-development, business development techniques and marketing enterprises. Mark speaks on several topics that enlighten, entertain and motivate his audiences to action!

Mark's Most Requested Topics/Programs:

- **My Adversity University**

  "Build Power, Credibility and Respect from Life's Lessons"

- **Champion Your Success**

  "Achieve What You Believe, Believe What You Can Achieve'

- **7-Secrets of Business Success**

  "The Keys to Wealth and Freedom"

- **Leadership**

  "From Ability to Credibility"

Schedule Mark to Speak at Your Next Event!

Mark Zupo

Contact us: 1-678-640-0585

*"Own your dreams and
plan your success."*
Mark Zupo - 2010

About the Author

Mark Zupo is an "Accomplished Entrepreneur" who has devoted his life to helping others to be successful in their goals and dreams. Mark is a highly-successful e-Business veteran and the Director of the JumpStart Learn And Earn System Institute™ teaching people how to make a full-time income from blogging and Internet marketing through his JumpStart™ Internet Marketing Mentoring Program.

Mark is a believer in the Internet's ability to deliver "life-changing" opportunity to anyone who finds a niche there. Mark's goal is to help you fulfill your career goals and achieve financial freedoms or independence managing a successful Virtual Internet business. Because he has worked in the ecommerce business, his consulting and e-Business acumen remains unequaled as an _Entrepreneurial Authority_.

Mark is a leader, and entrepreneur and a mentor to many.

Mark hails from Pittsburgh, PA. Mark has long been

an entrepreneur and small business advocate and aviation enthusiast. He holds a commercial pilot's License as well as a Flight Instructor certificate teaching in multi-engine, turbine aircraft. A past aerobatic pilot, mark has flown many different aircraft across the world for business and pleasure. His favorite place to fly is New Zealand where he hopes to return to someday.

Mark says, "I'm a kid at heart! I believe in having a good time and hard work too. In fact, maybe I like hard work a little too much! I'm fortunate to have an unbelievably supportive family and many interesting friends. I've been involved with aviation, IT and ecommerce my entire life. I've been described as a "work-a-holic-serial-entrepreneur." I have been fortunate to have realized almost all of my dreams.

"Make Your Business Your Life and Make Your Life Your Business!"

Mark Zupo

A note from Mark

First I would like to say thank you for your trust.

I know there is a world of options out there but you chose to read my book. That is a very humbling and special thing for me.

I am an entrepreneur who has published books, created online home study courses, created digital information books, mentor, trained and presented at various seminars both in-person and online. For the past 24 years I have been actively involved with mentoring in the success-motivation industry.

As a thought-leader and business mentor I have worked with businesses and people all over the world. I have worked with educators, business owners, individuals, entrepreneurs, lawyers, consultants, coaches, trainers and more. As founder of the ***7-Level Success Academy*®** I have helped these same people achieve personal and business success, improvement to life and happiness.

Maybe I can help you too.

Achieve what you can believe

On-line: *www.MarkZupo.com*
markzupo@gmail.com

www.7LevelSuccess.com

Disclaimer

---The stuff that makes the lawyers happy.

Every effort has been made to make this report as complete and accurate as possible. However, there may be mistakes in typography or content. The purpose of this e-book is to educate. The author and the publisher does not warrant that the information contained in this e-book is fully complete and shall not be responsible for any errors or omissions. The author and publisher shall have neither liability nor responsibility to any person or entity with respect to any loss or damage caused or alleged to be caused directly or indirectly by this e-book

This information is not presented is for educational and informational purposes only and is not intended to be a substitute for professional advice. Never disregard professional advice or delay in seeking it because of something you have read or heard.

We make every effort to ensure that we accurately represent our products and services and their potential for income. Earning and Income statements made by our company and its customers are estimates of what we think you can possibly earn. There is no guarantee that you will make the level of income you desire and you accept the risk that the earnings and income statements differ by individual.

As with any business, your results may vary, and will be based on your individual capacity, business

experience, expertise, and level of desire. There are no guarantees concerning the level of success you may experience. The testimonials and examples used are exceptional results, which do not apply to the average purchaser, and are not intended to represent or guarantee that anyone will achieve the same or similar results. Each individual's success depends on his or her background, dedication, desire and motivation.

There is no assurance that examples of past earnings can be duplicated and we cannot guarantee your future results and/or success. There are unknown risks in business and on the internet that we cannot foresee which can reduce results. We are not responsible for your actions.

The use of our information, products and services should be based on your own due diligence and you hold harmless our company for any success or failure of your business that is directly or indirectly related to the purchase and use of our information, products and services.

Thank you for visiting or reading material from www.markzupo.com, 7LevelSuccess.com, yourfastbook.com or any and all affiliated websites or printed material. This represents the earnings Disclaimer from one of the above sites, referred to herein as "this web site", the "company", the "corporation, LLC". The products and services sold in any form printed, electronic, digital or audio on this web site or through private vendors are not to be interpreted as a promise or guarantee of earnings.

Your level of success in attaining the results from using our products and information depends on the time you devote to the program, ideas and techniques used, your finances, knowledge and various skills. Since these factors differ among each individual, we cannot guarantee your success or income level, nor are we responsible for any of your actions. Any and all forward-looking statements on this web site or in any of our products are intended to express our opinion of the earnings potential that some people may achieve. But many factors will be important in determining your actual results, and we make no guarantees that you will achieve results similar to ours or anyone else's. In fact, we make no guarantees that you will achieve any results from the ideas and techniques contained on our web site or in our products.

To the extent that we included any case studies or testimonials on this site, you can assume that none of these stories in any way represent the "average" or "typical" customer experience. In fact, as with any product or service, we know that some people will purchase our products but never use them at all, and therefore will get no results whatsoever. You should therefore assume that you will obtain no results with this program.

Even though we make no guarantees that our product will produce any particular result for you, you can still take advantage of our return policy if you are not completely satisfied. In such instances, you can return the product for a refund according to the terms and timelines indicated in our refund policy described in the Terms and Conditions section.

YOU FULLY AGREE AND UNDERSTAND THAT COMPANY IS NOT RESPONSIBLE FOR YOUR SUCCESS OR FAILURE AND MAKES NO REPRESENTATIONS OR WARRANTIES OF ANY KIND WHATSOEVER THAT OUR PRODUCTS OR SERVICES WILL PRODUCE ANY PARTICULAR RESULT FOR YOU.

NOTES -

NOTES -

Achieve what you can believe

NOTES -

NOTES -

www.ingramcontent.com/pod-product-compliance
Lightning Source LLC
Chambersburg PA
CBHW070951040426
42443CB00007B/460